Directing Amateur Theatre

Directing Amateur Theatre
A Professional Approach

Geoff Morris Michell

*WITH 29 WORKING ILLUSTRATIONS
BY THE AUTHOR*

Northcote House

Published by Northcote House Publishers Ltd,
Plymbridge House, Estover Road, Plymouth PL6 7PY, United Kingdom.
Tel: Plymouth (01752) 202368. Fax: (01752) 202330

ISBN 07463 0646 6

Typeset by PDQ Typesetting, Newcastle-under-Lyme
Printed and bound in the United Kingdom

Contents

Illustrations

A NOTE ON DIMENSIONS

In the later stage of transition from Imperial to Metric a measure of confusion is inevitable. This is particularly acute in the theatre. While constructional engineering, timber and other raw supplies come in Metric and Imperial, scenery suppliers and practising Stage Managers continue to think and work from stage plans drawn in feet and inches. So for those who may wish to construct items as suggested in these pages, I have indicated measurements in Metric and where appropriate in Imperial. For those planning the finished sets, I have retained the more readily visualised and familiar measurements. Plans and Setting lines are scaled in feet, with Flats in 4, 6 or 8ft widths, and Cloths and Tabs 20, 24 or 36ft as currently supplied.

G. M.M.

Preface

This book is primarily for those whose love of live drama draws them to active participation in the wide and dynamic field of amateur theatre. Enthusiasts will scarcely need reminding that the amateur is one who pursues a study or an art for the love of it. They will also know that there is some fine talent in the amateur field and that most professional theatre practitioners started as amateurs. This being so, there is every reason to suppose that the art should be cradled in loving excellence. And a great deal of it is. Why, then, is the word 'amateur' in this context often used in a somewhat pejorative sense?

There may be various reasons. One of them may have something to do with the difference between the noun 'amateur' and the adjective 'amateurish'. Despite the loving dedication the amateur, as an individual, brings to the endeavour, the collective effort may sometimes remain stubbornly amateurish. Why should this be so?

From a long experience which has included almost every aspect of live performance and production, both in professional and amateur theatre, I believe the answer lies in the area of presentation. While exceptional art will shine through indifferent framing, even modest talent may be greatly enhanced by careful display and presentation. And it is precisely this aspect which is the concern of this book. The aim is to set out for the inexperienced some of the methods and practices of the professional theatre by which, with a moderate amount of trouble, the amateur production may be given a professional polish.

The first aim of any work of art is to achieve a unity. No more so than in the theatre, where this is accomplished most effectively by vesting the overall vision of the production in one person. How that person acquires such a responsible position will depend on a variety of circumstances. He or she may be the moving spirit in an aspiring group, or perhaps be invited to undertake the task in recognition of proven ability. Enjoying the confidence of the company, and sure of his competence, this person will co-ordinate the multifarious efforts of the whole group into a coherent whole, giving direction to the whole proceeding. Thus he will, in fact, be the Director. In a similar manner, to give shape and coherence to the many aspects of theatre production, this book is written from the Director's overall point of view.

The theatre is a meeting place of all the arts and many crafts and, in this context, they have become highly specialised fields. It is unlikely that anyone could master them all. Those who would specialise in one or more aspects will find an extensive range of books, literature, courses and summer schools available, some of which are indicated at the end of this book. Their real value, however, can only be fully understood and appreciated if accompanied by practical experience. For that, amateur theatre makes an invaluable grounding.

One of the outstanding demands of, in particular, modern musical theatre is smoothness, speed and pace of presentation, summed up in the word 'flow'. Reinforced by the emphasis it receives in television and cinema, to which, by its ready accessibility to the public at large, the general expectation is ever more sharply geared, people almost unconsciously now come to expect a standard of slick presentation markedly different from older methods and times. Recent plays and musicals themselves are intensively geared to this expectation as a comparison of contemporary productions with those of a few years ago will instantly show.

The proposition embedded in this book is that the achievement of flow requires a greater degree of skill in the manipulation of practical stagecraft than is often apparent in amateur theatre. Clearly the impetus to achieve a high degree of presentation must come from the person whose vision guides the production. That is the Director. It requires a knowledge of the physical possibilities and limitations of stage and lighting equipment, both general and specific to local circumstances.

This book attempts to show how the concept of flow has to be integrated into the planning of the production from the very start. With the emphasis on practical stagecraft, it lists the information required; shows how to obtain it; and then how to process it to form a visual base from which the organisation of staging, lighting, and rehearsals, both in the rehearsal room and in the theatre, can proceed to achieve the best results. Examples of plans, plots, schedules and schemes actually used are provided in illustrations.

Lighting plays an increasingly important part in modern presentation and there are two chapters devoted to it. A brief theoretical section in Part One leads to a survey of lighting facilities available. In Part Two lighting design for the amateur includes planning, positioning, plotting and control of lighting throughout the production.

The book is in two parts. Part One considers some of the attributes one might look for in a Director and offers a guide to the practical aspects of stagecraft, including the construction, painting and working of scenery and how the stage operates, and describes the technical personnel and the parts they play in a quite complicated process. Open stage techniques are discussed and suggestions and detailed plans for a do-it-yourself system of staging for drama groups is included.

Part Two concentrates on how the Director makes use of the skills and resources described in Part One in order to shape a production. To be comprehensive, the staging of a musical play is chosen as an example of production method. This will include all the aspects of staging a play, plus many other important aspects of direction.

The contemporary amateur society's problems in presenting the fast eighteen or twenty scene modern integrated musical frequently in circumstances far from ideal – on stages which come to an abrupt end eighteen inches behind the last drape, or where flying facilities for all practical purposes are virtually non-existent – are not ignored. A resourceful imagination and the use of lateral thinking are essential in such cases. From just such experiences, I have included practical suggestions and ways of overcoming difficulties which, with a little do-it-yourself endeavour, should be well within the province of the keen society.

To avoid the tedious, repeated phrase 'he or she', it should be understood (of course) that wherever the Director is referred to as 'he' it could just as well be 'she' – this also applies to the posts of Stage Manager, Designer, Electrician, etc. In the same way, the Wardrobe Mistress may well be a Wardrobe Master, the Property Master may well be a Property Mistress, and so on.

G. M. M.

Acknowledgements

I should like to express my appreciation for the help I have received in the preparation of this book. To John L. Hughes for reading the manuscript and for helpful comments. To the electrician, whose idea of lighting board plotting I adapted to create the system described and have used successfully, but whose identity, unfortunately, I have not been able to establish. (This, despite the help of Andy Collier of Strand Lighting, who explored the Tabs archives on my behalf.) To my editor, Neil Dowden, for his perceptive suggestions. Lastly, and by no means least, to my wife whose typing, help in the preparation of the index, and support throughout has been of immense value. Any mistakes or omissions are, of course, mine.

PART ONE
Stagecraft

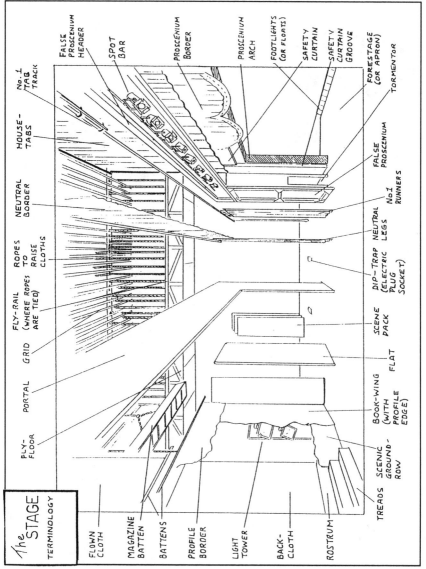

Illustration 1: Stage Terminology

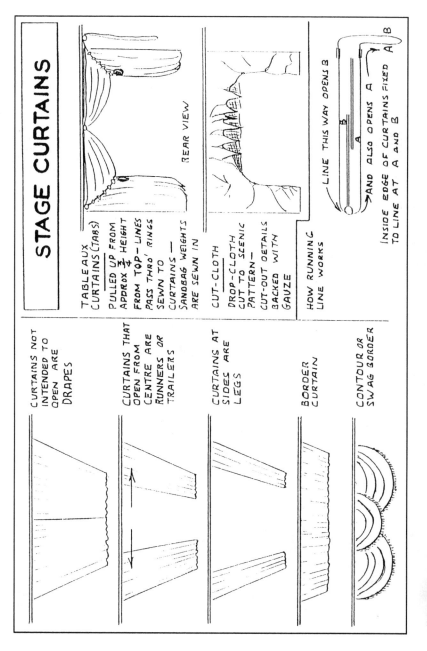

Illustration 2: Stage curtains

1 | *The Director*

What does he do?

Since early in the century the roles of Producer and Director have been redefined. It is generally accepted now that the Producer is the person who is responsible for putting the whole package together. He decides what production to mount, chooses the performers and the theatre and finds the resources to back the project. He engages a Director to take charge and be responsible for bringing all the various elements together on stage. In this context, it is the society or drama group who is the producer, and the 'Producer' they appoint to co-ordinate the production becomes the 'Director'. Traditions are slow to change and in many quarters the Director habitually remains 'the Producer'. In these pages, however, 'Director' is used as defined above.

So what is the function of the Director? What does he actually do?

To the uninitiated the task of the Director is obscure. Something to do with sitting with the script and telling the actors which side they come on from and to speak up. In some quarters there may even be the belief enunciated by Bernard Shaw that those who can, do, while those who cannot tell others what to do. Indeed, there have been instances in amateur drama where enthusiastic aspiration, unsustained by technical know-how, has given the old adage more than a degree of truth.

There are Directors who favour the 'inspirational' school of directing, who believe that creativity arises with greater effect in the heat of the rehearsal moment. This may be true for some, and it can be much more fun for all if rehearsals are spread over lengthy periods of experimentation.

However, a common complaint is that some Directors start rehearsals without knowing which side the players enter from, or where they should go when they do come on. Some have also directed the first act in a manner that, to the dismay of the players, has completely falsified the action in the second act. Other Directors do their homework!

Whichever way is favoured, that success is compounded of one tenth inspiration and nine tenths perspiration is a sentiment with which all who work in the theatre would unhesitatingly agree. Ultimately, however, it is the Director's task to lead and quite literally give direction to clothing the vision in hand with theatrical reality.

An aesthetic appreciation is, of course, only a part of the successful Director's armoury. He (or she) must also be capable of giving practical expression to visionary concepts, and this in turn requires a knowledge of the practical possibilities and limitations of the medium. To this must be added the capability of conveying his ideas to others clearly and unambiguously. In short, in addition to his other attributes he must be capable of organising.

It should be borne in mind that the heart of directing is necessarily a subjective affair, guided and conditioned by personal knowledge, artistic sensibility and experience. That essential spark is best kindled by a working knowledge of the medium, and it is just this with which this book is most concerned. Part One considers the Director's role, the areas in which he works, and attempts to define the qualifications and qualities it is desirable he should possess. Part Two follows the Director as he makes use of the processes outlined in Part One in preparing the production from start to finish.

The Director's function as artist

First and foremost, it is assumed that the Director starts out as an artist. That is to say, he is possessed of artistic sensibilities and that they are, in the main, orientated to the theatre. In short, he has a love of live performance in the theatre.

The work of the Director, at its most basic, is the work of translation. From a starting point of symbols on paper, his task is to translate, to transform, those symbols into a 'larger than life', living performance, so as to convey the message of those symbols in a way that can be understood as clearly and unequivocally as possible by the spectator. The symbols on paper may be a simple poem, a song (in which case there will be two sets of symbols – words and music), or the manuscript of a musical production.

What the Director needs is the capacity to read the text, the bare print in such a way that the act of reading becomes no longer a conscious activity, but is subsumed into a visual representation of the meaning, the situation and the characters involved. The mental picture will not necessarily be derived purely from the text. It will be fleshed out and amplified by the reader's past perceptions.

The Director must have the ability to create images of scenes, light and colour, and to imagine sounds, voices and music. The term 'to create' with its suggestion of a conscious activity, may not be an accurate description of what happens since, in fact, it doesn't work like that. The images arise spontaneously from an active imagination. And if there is a love of theatre, the images will occur as if seen on a stage. This kind of imagination is the Director's most vital asset.

There are many ways he comes into possession of the symbols on paper. He may be presented with a script, a play, in the course of his profession, or he may come across a story in some other way and develop a burning desire to give it expression, in which case he may become part Producer. In whatever way he acquires the text, his treatment of it is likely to follow a broadly similar pattern.

He will study the text and gain from it certain impressions. His imagination will then clothe these initial impressions in pictorial representations. He may visualise certain parts of it quite vividly, sensing the characters and the situation surrounding them. Then he may well build up in his mind the whole conceptual line, the meaning, and perhaps the message as expressed and portrayed through the characters the dramatist or author has created. He will see with his mind's eye, informed by the possibilities offered by the medium, the events and the characters, in shades of colour and in degrees of light and shade, and also in terms of scenic surround, position and movement. From his understanding of the text, and his imaginative response to it, he will build his own conception and, through the initial planning of all the elements involved, the physical shape of the production will begin to emerge and soon a vision will form of the whole thing brought to life on stage.

Communication skills

Unlike the painter, sculptor or writer, the Director works at one or more removes from the finished product. That is to say, he works through other people. It is the skills of actors, technicians, artists, musicians, costumiers, etc., that he relies on to give substance to his vision. It is important, therefore, that he must be able to express clearly his intentions and requirements. In short, he must be able to communicate.

To communicate ideas successfully requires clarity of thought and the ability to organise that thinking into the variety of channels relevant to the various groups of people he relies on and in a manner they will understand. This means that with the artistic proclivity there will be an analytical trait. He will be able to sort out the various strands that make up the atmosphere, the mood or the impact of a particular scene in so far as they affect the different departments involved. He will know the position, the tone of voice and the posture of the actor, the scenic environment, the quality of light and how and when it will vary, the value of sound and silence, and the pace, feeling and volume of music if it is involved. The Director should therefore be able to communicate clearly within all these elements.

Knowledge of Stagecraft
The Actor

It is of great help if the Director himself has experience as an actor or performing artiste. The more experience the better since he will know the strains and stresses that are the accompaniment of the actor's technique: the basic skill of memorising the lines and the problems of character creation. At the very least he will know what it is reasonable to ask of him.

He will know from experience that over-long rehearsals can sometimes be counter-productive. He will sense just when the actor or the company have had enough of a particular session. In other words, he will be able to talk to the actor in his own language.

Costume

If he himself has worn costumes, he will have a sympathetic understanding of how costumes can help or hinder the performer. A well-fitting costume can go a long way to project the kind of character the actor is aiming for. Conversely, a costume that is too tight, too loose or in some other way a source of annoyance, can throw the actor off his lines or divert his attention from the portrayal of his character. The Director should be able to match the costumes to the characters, the situations, and the moods of the scenes. Colour sense is a part of this, as is also a sense of style. He may not be able to make costumes, but should be able to choose pictures, drawings or photographs which will help him convey the kind of costumes required. If he can sketch outlines of what he has in mind, he will communicate even more effectively with the designer or costumier.

Make-up

As noted elsewhere, all aspects of theatrical art have achieved specialised status. The close scrutiny of the close-up lens in cinema and television has elevated make-up to a very high point of technical expertise. While this has had an influence in the theatre, it is unlikely that the Director will share such specialised techniques. Nevertheless, as in other respects, it is as well if he has an understanding of the basics in so far as stage make-up is concerned.

This is one aspect of theatre with which he can explore and experiment completely on his own, without having to rely on anyone else's cooperation. There is no better way of getting to know this subject than by actually doing. There are many books available and the basic advice on the subject in this book will prove a good starting point. As in other aspects, make-up artistry should never look forced. The secret of good make-up is when the effect is achieved mainly by the response of facial expression and bodily movement to the imagination and feeling for the character. The attention of the spectator should not be diverted from the character to the make-up.

Scenery

The scenery assists in the creation of location and period, suggesting an historic and social environment. It is the framework that adds meaning to the effort of actors, dramatists and directors. It can create mood, add symbolism, and also lend variety, novelty and pace. In the latter, especially in musical productions, the Designer or Director is able to do a great deal – an aspect dealt with at some length in Chapter 9, Groundwork, Chapter 10, Groundwork Continued, and Chapter 13, Flow, in Part Two.

It is extremely useful if the Director can make sketches, even water-colours, of what he has in mind. If he knows the practical side of sets, scenery and stagecraft and can prepare scale drawings of proposed settings, however rudimentary, he will be able to talk intelligently to the Scenic Designer or contractor.

Lighting

Lighting is perhaps the most important item in the Director's armoury in creating mood, directing attention and establishing atmosphere. He should, therefore, be somewhat phototropic. That is, like plants and animals, he should respond to the colour, quality and intensity of light, and be aware of the debilitating effect of dimness and the heightened tone of brilliant light.

Next to music, lighting is probably the most potent way of engendering emotional response. To be able to realise its immense potential, the Director should know something of the means by which the desired effects may be attained. He should have at least an acquaintance with the array of different lantern types, their uses and how these may be controlled.

Sound

A myriad different sources combine to make a blanket of sound that envelopes us for a great deal of our daily lives, so much so that many people feel uneasy in silence and hastily turn on the radio, for example, as a measure of reassurance that they are not alone. There is an over-use of sound in much television drama and it would be unfortunate indeed if this kind of saturation were to invade the theatre. Unfortunate, because music and sound, if used sparingly, have a great deal more dramatic effect then a continuous onslaught of sound.

Apart from opera and ballet where music is of prime consideration, the theatre centres mainly on the spoken word and anything that detracts from it is unwelcome. This is not to deny that music or sound have a part to play. Sound effects can be used to create the illusion of activities that would be difficult to portray on stage, such as bird-song, car crashes, bomb explosions and the noise of crowds, rain and so on. Music may be used to create atmosphere, emphasise dramatic highlights and evoke moods. The essential thing is that it be used with discretion and never allowed to obtrude. In musicals themselves, to some extent, there is a built-in balance between musical numbers and the spoken word. In other presentations it is the judgement of the Director that will maintain a proper balance.

Dealing with people

In attending to all these aspects of production, the Director will be dealing with people: actors, designers, musicians, artists and technicians. Amateur or professional, they will all have different points of view, temperaments and thresholds of tolerance. It is desirable therefore that the Director should be able to deal with people, both one-to-one and in groups. He will be relying on them to do what he wants. How he goes about this will be governed by his own approach and the prevailing circumstances. Usually people respond to a tactful, friendly approach more easily than to demands. This is true both for the professional and the amateur Director. The professional often has the ultimate sanction of dismissal at times of acute disagreement, but not always. The star name may have greater pull with the Producer and the box-office. There is a well-known apocryphal story of Dame Edith Evans, discussing some bit of business with her fellow actors, turning to a rather zealous young Director with a withering 'Do be quiet young man, we'll get around to you later'.

In the amateur field the Director must always remember that the people he is dealing with are there for the love of it. They give their time and far from being paid, they often pay a subscription to take part. There is no place in these circumstances for over-imperious commands.

What people, both professional and amateur, respond to most readily is the person who has a clear idea of what he wants, can explain that idea and can communicate to the different groups of people concerned *in their own terms*. If he can do this, while respecting their own individual expertise, artistic or technical, and can convince them that he knows his subject, they will respect his judgement and respond favourably.

It is for this reason that the Director should add to his artistic judgement as wide and as thorough a knowledge of practical stagecraft as he can possibly manage. Just as actual experience of acting is of inestimable value to the Director, so too is similar experience of practical stagecraft. Here again, he will know what is and what is not possible.

Technical know-how

It may be pertinent to note that while a general grasp of theatre practice as advocated here is highly desirable, the Director, while perhaps specialising in some particular aspect of production, need not, however, be a specialist in all fields (even if it were possible nowadays). But he should know in what direction to look for specialist help when necessary.

To stimulate and encourage experiment, the rest of Part One of this book is devoted to a review of the nitty-gritty of practical stagecraft. With this background knowledge, as it were, absorbed in his mind, the aspiring Director will then be able to translate his study of the current production into actual stage events. In short, he will learn to 'THINK THEATRE!'

2 | Stage-Management

Who does what?

In maintaining overall charge of the production, the Director should have a general knowledge of the mechanics of the stage if for no other reason than to know what is and what is not possible. To meet the demands of modern production, backstage is an area of increasing technological development. Some understanding of the relevant terms used and its general working will enable him, at least, to communicate intelligibly. To this end, a cursory survey of the stage-management field, the personnel involved and their separate spheres of action may prove useful.

The Stage-Manager

As the title implies, the Stage-Manager is the one in charge of the stage. His function is to make sure that the stage, the scenery, the flies and all the appurtenances connected with it, including the personnel, are working efficiently and effectively in presenting the show. He is responsible for the correct setting of all the scenes, the smooth changes and the safety of all concerned (the stage can sometimes be a dangerous place). While he may assist in the scene changes, ideally, he should not be tied to any specific duty. Rather he should be available to attend to any emergency should it arise. While his authority is unchallengeable, particularly during the performance, he does not actually 'run' the performance. That is the function of the Deputy Stage-Manager (see page 32).

If the Stage-Manager is a non-professional with an established drama group, such as a school, college or 'Little Theatre Society', it is very likely that he will have attended preliminary conferences with the Director or Designer – indeed, perhaps in the majority of cases he will *be* the Designer. He is also likely, with the not unimportant matter of economy of resources in mind, to be able to envisage the alteration and transformation of existing scenic stock to the new requirements. In any event, he will, as far as the stage is concerned, be the one to give practical reality to the Director's concept. He is, therefore, an important ally. A good reason for knowing something of his sphere of activity.

He is likely to be a practical man, with some skill in, or at very least an elementary knowledge of, woodworking. In the professional theatre he has often been the Stage-Carpenter. In amateur circles it is very likely that he will be useful with tools and know how to handle a paint brush.

The difference between the amateur Stage-Manager and the professional Stage-Manager is, perhaps, a matter of scale. It will be useful, therefore, to take a look at how a production is set up in a typical working theatre, noting key people and the parts they play. First, those most occupied with the actual construction; then, the functions of those, equally important, who contribute to the running of the production.

One of the first things the Stage-Manager will have already done is to have studied the plans of the sets and the proposed 'hanging plot' (see page 87) provided earlier by the Director, and he will thus be in a position to raise any queries or problems at an early stage. Having dealt with this, his next concern will be to prepare the stage to receive the production, which in practical terms means arranging the 'get-in'.

The 'Get-in'

This means arranging to get the scenery from the scenic contractor's lorries onto the stage. In the case of an amateur society this may be only a matter of receiving the flats and scenery (with which he may already be familiar) from the workshop into the theatre.

He will already have cleared the stage as much as possible, as well as the 'grid', i.e. the system of pulleys over the stage from which the scenery is suspended, ready to receive the incoming items. He will also, hopefully, have arranged enough men to handle it all.

During the 'get-in', his most useful function is to station himself at the scene-dock doors and do his best to identify the various items, indicating where he wants them placed. He will watch the battened backcloths and note which way they are rolled, so that they will be carried on stage with the visible batten upstage ready to be attached to the lines, thus avoiding the waste of time involved in 'circusing' cloths which would otherwise be carried in back-to-front. He will be watching the flats to see which are marked O/P and which P/S (see Glossary) and will have them placed in the appropriate packs. Vigilance here can save much re-handling later on.

The 'Fit-up'

Next comes the 'fit-up', i.e. the hanging of those items which will be lowered in from the flies and the disposition in appropriate places around the stage of the flats, rostra, ground-rows and other pieces making up the scenic environment of the production.

Working in accordance with the 'hanging plot', with the assistance of three or four stage-hands and the fly-floor staff, he will then get all the backdrops, borders and similar items 'flown', i.e. fixed to battens, (which are themselves attached to sets of lines) and pulled up overhead out of sight above the borders.

As each cloth, drape or border is raised, the Stage-Manager, consulting the 'hanging-plot', will call to the Head Fly-man the numbers of the scenes in which the items will be used, e.g.: 'Bar 24. Mark that 5 and 18.' This, means that Bar 24, from which the item is suspended, will be lowered in as part of scene 5 and scene 18.

The Stage-Manager will also 'dead' (see Glossary) the items hung from the battens or counter-weighted bars, either after each one is attached, or sometimes after they are all hung, when he will have them lowered one by one and proceed with this task. It consists in seeing that each cloth, drape, etc., is correctly hung and, where it makes contact with the stage, is level all the width of the cloth and touches the stage without portions folding over, thus causing wrinkles or folds. In a counter-weight system this problem is largely taken care of mechanically with the adjustable chains.

However, in the rope and pulley system the batten will be suspended by three individual ropes, so the Stage-Manager may, for example, be heard calling to the Fly-men above holding on to the ropes: 'Take up the centre line. In a little on the "short" [i.e the shortest line – the one running over the pulley nearest them.] Hold it there. In a little on the "long". [i.e. the longest line – the one running over the pulley at the other side of the stage.] Right. Tie off there and don't lose any.' This means that the cloth is hanging level, that the ropes should be tied around the cleat without letting any of them in any further.

In shows which have a great deal of scenery (a pantomime perhaps), the Director might prepare a schema or chart for the guidance of the Stage-Manager and the Fly-men. It will list the scenes and the sets of lines required for each (see Illustration 3 on page 29).

In control of the fly-floor, usually a gallery raised above the stage level, from which the raising and lowering of all the drapes, scenery, borders and all that is flown above the stage is operated, is the Head Fly-man.

The Head Fly-man

During the hanging process as described, in accordance with the instructions of the Stage-Manager, the Head Fly-man will mark on a blackboard the sequence of scenes and the number of sets of lines appropriate to each. Where the ropes holding the cloth are 'tied off' on

No.	SCENE	BORDER	MARKET CUT CLOTH	STREET	TERRACE	GARDEN CUT	MARKET CUT	GARDEN B/DROP	MARKET B/DROP	GAUZE	SKY	ETC →
		(LINE NUMBERS)										
		1	2	3	4	5	6	7	8	9	10	ETC →
1	MARKET	1	2				6		8			
2	GARDEN	1				5		7				
3	STREET	1		3								
4	MARKET	1	2				6		8			
5	TERRACE	1			4			7				
6	HEATH	1								9	10	

ETC
↓

Illustration 3: Flies Working Schema
Thus Scene 1 requires Bars 1, 2, 6, and 8 Scene 2 requires Bars 1, 5, 7 and so on.
From this schema the Head Fly-man can quickly see which lines may be preset. e.g.
if stage setting allows, lines 9 and 10 could be preset from Scene 1.

the cleat will constitute the cloth's bottom 'dead'. Sometimes, for a different scene, the cloth may be repeated but at a different 'dead'. To facilitate this, the second 'dead' is established and a piece of tape is tied around the ropes opposite the level of the fly-rail, thus indicating the second 'dead'.

Where the flying is accomplished with ropes, this is known as a 'hemp' system (see Glossary) and there will be three, four or more additional Fly-men, according to the size and speed of the show. A full cloth will need two or three men to haul up and 'tie-off' the ropes around the cleat on the fly-rail. It is not an easy task for the men holding the weight of the cloth and sorting out the centre, the long or the short lines, when the ropes are all bunched together in their hands. In well-run theatres, to assist the Fly-men, the hemp lines may be coloured, one colour for the long line, another colour for the centre, and the short left neutral.

A counter-weight system will require fewer men, since the weight of each cloth is counter-balanced in a mechanical system, which allows the raising and lowering of each cloth to be operated by one man, who has simply to apply a brake to hold the cloth at the required height.

Wing-men

In a production involving much scene changing, the Stage-Manager will ensure he has enough men on each side of the stage to cope with striking and setting. There will usually be two experienced 'day-men', i.e. men employed on a full-time basis who will have assisted in the 'get-in' and 'fit-up' and will, during the performance, be stationed one on each side, in charge of the O/P and P/S stage-hands. These are the No 1 Wing-men. They and their teams will, in the main, attend to all the setting items stored on their side of the stage, co-operating with the opposite side when necessary. The No 1 Wing-men will usually arrange that each man in his team performs the same task at each strike and set. This avoids confusion and helps enormously in smooth working.

'Masking'

If the Director or Designer has done his desk-work thoroughly, the Stage-Manager will be considerably assisted in his next problem: 'Masking'. This means masking from the view of the audience those areas side-stage where the edges of the backdrop, off-stage edges of wing-pieces and flats may otherwise be seen. From the plans he will have seen which scenes are self-masking and which may require neutral flats or neutral legs. In the latter case, he will make sure he has enough available. He will also check from the auditorium that borders are at the correct height to mask above the stage (see Illustration 10, Sight Lines, on page 85).

The Stage-Manager will establish his scene 'packs'. In other words, he will place the wing-pieces, flats, and so on, in packs, both O/P and P/S as appropriate, so that the ones used first will be on top. He will arrange space by the side of the pack so that as each piece is used, it will be placed in a second used pack – in reverse. When the performance is over the used pack will be put back into its original place and once again reversed, so that it is ready for the next performance.

Where quick changes, perhaps involving trucks, revolves, flippers and the like, are required (as they are in most modern musicals), it is useful to prepare a 'stage action plot' for the Stage-Manager showing the changes involved. From this he will usually prepare copies for each side of the stage for the guidance of his stage crew and for the Property Master.

If the production is a play, with perhaps one standing set, the Stage-Manager might then proceed to build the set, ready for the Director's inspection. If the production has lots of scenes, this will probably be left to a later date when the Electrician and his crew have set up the lighting in accordance with the 'lighting-rig plot', (see page 120).

Time is the important factor here. In some amateur groups the stage may be available for a week or more, in which case the sets may be erected on different occasions and the Electrician given time to position and focus the lanterns. There may even be the luxury of allowing the actors to rehearse in the sets. In the professional theatre, and where societies hire a theatre, it will often mean tight scheduling, and the Electricians coming in to rig the lighting when the stage crew have finished, or perhaps between building sessions, or overnight.

To facilitate setting, the Stage-Manager will see that the set or sets are marked on the stage, usually with paint at the 'knuckles' (corners) and ends of flats, with corner marks for rostra and treads. He will use different colours for different scenes. He will take frequent looks from the auditorium to check the masking of each set, both side-stage and above.

The Electrician

As the title implies, the Electrician is in control of all electrical installations. As stage lighting has steadily increased in importance, so has the role of the Electrician. In the professional theatre the disposition and use of the lighting equipment may be decided by the Lighting Designer (who may be a hired expert, or the Director), but it is the Electrician who is responsible for the actual work of placing the lanterns, according to the 'rig-plot' drawn up.

He will work in close co-operation with whoever designs the lighting, since he has knowledge of the particular theatre installation, its circuitry, facilities and loading. He will usually have one or more assistants, especially when hanging or focussing the lanterns. While someone is up a ladder (or, if lucky, on the platform of a 'Tallescope', a mobile ladder) positioning the lanterns, to save time, there must be someone on the control board to switch on each lantern as required.

During the performance it may be the Chief Electrician who works the control panel or board, or sometimes he deputes this to an assistant, leaving himself free to keep a supervisory position over controls and effects and changes on stage.

The Deputy Stage-Manager

Generally the Stage-Manager and Electrician are employed by the theatre, while the Deputy Stage-Manager, on the other hand, is a member of the producing company. During the setting up of the production, he will keep a keen eye on the construction and rigging of the lighting to see that it will adhere to the Director's conception, and facilitate the sequence of scenes and effects as demanded by the cues in his prompt book.

So that the Stage-Manager is free to give his attention anywhere on stage as required, it is the Deputy Stage-Manager who 'runs the corner'. And 'running the corner' means being in charge of the performances. The 'corner' is usually a space downstage immediately behind the P/S tormentor, from where the Deputy Stage-Manager can have a clear view of the stage.

He will have a little desk or shelf on which to place the prompt book and time sheet. Somewhere above, there will be a clock. There is likely to be a number of switches and buttons for controlling pilot lights, and warning lights to the flies, the orchestra, below stage and the O/P side of the stage. There will also probably be a microphone which he will use to give the warning time-calls through the backstage and dressing-rooms sound system. There may be a tape-deck for sound effects too. Most importantly, he will don a talk-back head-set, consisting of microphone and ear-piece, through which he can communicate to flies, the Electrician, follow-spot operators, the O/P side and perhaps the orchestra conductor (though this is sometimes a separate telephone).

In some shows with complicated staging, the Deputy Stage-Manager will be equipped with a mobile desk fitted with all the necessary cueing equipment which can be moved up and down stage to the position from where he can best see the action on stage. Walkie-talkies are also used at times between heads of departments and the Deputy Stage-Manager.

The Deputy Stage-Manager is responsible for making sure the show starts on time, cueing all concerned in running the performance, timing the scenes, (to make sure it all runs to schedule), and supervising curtain up and curtain calls at the end. It is an exacting job requiring a thorough knowledge of the show, close co-operation with the Director in the preparation of the prompt book and constant attention throughout each performance. The Deputy Stage-Manager should never leave the 'corner' unsupervised. He must be on the look-out at all times for the untoward incident. The responsibility involved calls for calmness and an alert intelligence.

The Deputy Stage-Manager will also note in the prompt book any changes made during the run, perhaps by the Director. These will usually be incorporated in succeeding productions of the play or show.

The Property Master

The Property Master's job is also a most exacting one – particularly in plays where there are interior sets having furniture with drawers containing papers, jewellery, guns and such like, all important to the action. He is responsible for dressing the set with cushions, ornaments and similar impedimenta as required. He is also in charge of all hand-props which the actors take on with them. Often the players like to look after their own hand-props in which case, because it is his responsibility, he usually checks that they haven't forgotten them before their entrance.

To enable him to fulfil all that is expected of him, he will have been supplied with a property plot listing the acts and scenes, the props required for each, the sides from which they are taken on and by whom. Hand-props will be listed for each character. With an amateur company, study of the script and listing of the properties required may also be his job, as well as buying, borrowing, hiring and otherwise acquiring them. He will attend rehearsals to note other requirements and when and where they are used.

Ideally there will be a corner of the scene dock, or somewhere on the stage, where big props can be stored and, importantly, a large trestle table, marked out with spaces corresponding to the scenes, in which will be placed the smaller props appropriate to each. He will very probably have the property list pinned on the table against which to check the items as they are set and returned.

It goes without saying that in many instances he will require assistants for quick set changes or to be ready off-stage to hand props to actors entering from which ever side is necessary. Often underrated, the job can be both tedious and demanding. The Property Master is often a key figure at rehearsals and certainly during performances.

Assistant Stage-Managers

One or more Assistant Stage-Managers are sometimes found with productions – usually plays. Often they are budding actors or actresses gaining experience, combining off-stage duties with walk-on parts. They will sometimes function as Property Masters, Deputy Stage-Managers, and undertake other duties as may be required.

The Tab-man

A word about the Tab-man. A good Tab-man is worth a great deal. His function is to open or close the running curtains, operate the wypes, either with the use of winches or hand-over-hand use of running lines. What makes a good Tab-man is his artistic sensibility. He can ruin the atmosphere of a scene by either opening or closing the tabs too quickly or too slowly. A good man will sense the atmosphere of a scene and judge the speed of the tabs so that they meet right at the end of the closing note of a song, or judge the length of a pause that gives meaning to a silent look. The Director can indicate a count, but someone imbued with sensitivity will interpret the cue with an intelligence and understanding not to be under-valued.

The Company Manager

For the sake of completing the off-stage personnel, a word about the Company Manager. With the professional production, he is the producing management's representative and in charge of the whole company. Often he combines this with the post of Stage-Director, with responsibility for the overall presentation. He deals with the business side, pays salaries, keeps the show running to time and up to scratch. He rehearses understudies, deals with the theatre management and makes all the arrangements for rehearsal rooms and, if touring, transporting the production. He also deals, at times, with the Musicians' Union, Equity and the Broadcasting, Entertainment, Cinematograph Theatre Union (BECTU), as well as the thousand and one problems that arise with artistes, chorus and staff during the run.

It is a job calling for some skill at figures, an eye for publicity opportunities, tact and a lot of patience. In the amateur theatre, his job will probably be split up and done by a number of committees or individuals like the society's Business Manager who, during performance times, may also double as Front-of-House Manager. There will probably also be an Honorary Treasurer and committees for programmes, publicity and other departments.

3 | Scenery

How to make and paint

Making scenery for the professional theatre is a specialised job, taking into account the requirements of flying, the possibility of touring and the robustness of the cloths and flats required to stand up to the strain of loading, unloading, repeated construction and pulling down. However for the amateur theatre, there is no reason why, given an elementary skill in woodwork and a modicum of artistic ability, satisfactory results may not be obtained by those willing to devote a little time and patience to building their own scenery.

Certainly there is an immense amount of satisfaction in designing and creating the setting for a play or other production, not to mention the financial advantages of a theatrical do-it-yourself exercise; especially if, as will be shown (in Chapter 4, Minimal Staging) there are ways of making ingenious units capable of repeated use for other productions.

What is offered first in this chapter are basic instructions and hints on the making of simple flats, well able to stand up to the more limited requirements of amateur production. It is hoped that the Director, Designer and Stage-Manager, as well as the society treasurer, may find inspiration in the following ideas.

Making Flats

On the principle that one picture is worth a thousand words, as a preliminary, it is recommended that the illustrations provided on pages 38 and 39, are studied since they demonstrate the basic techniques involved. The comments here are intended to supplement the drawings.

Use 50mm x 25mm timber. Undressed timber may be quite satisfactory if you can manage to smooth it sufficiently for easy handling. It is cheaper than that supplied dressed or finished. (You can use 45mm x 20mm timber but the resulting flats may not stand up to repeated handling or last so long).

Simple half-lap joints are adequate, provided they are also firmly glued and screwed. ⅞in counter-sunk wood screws are suitable. Pearl fish-glue is probably cheapest, but you will need a glue pot (a double container, with water in the outer container to boil the glue in the inner – an old saucepan large enough to contain a tin with the glue in will make a good substitute). A gas ring to boil it on is favourite, but alternative means may be tried. If facilities do not permit, one of the newer wood adhesives may be used instead.

Corners and middle support bars jointed in should be similarly fixed; for extra stability reinforce with triangles of hardboard, approximately 5in x 5in on the right-angle sides. Use 1in copper hardboard pins to fix in position. Instead of hardboard, 3mm plywood can be used but may be more expensive.

Dimensions

Other than the width and thickness of timber used, no other dimensions are given. The height of the flats will be governed by the height at which borders are set on the particular stage where they are to be used. It is unlikely that the flats will be less than 10ft – this is a reasonable and convenient height for smaller stages, with the borders set a few inches below the top of the flats. 4ft wide is a standard width for flats, though on some stages with limited depth 3ft may be sufficient. In the latter case, an exception would have to be made for a door flat. This would have to be 4ft wide to allow a door 2ft 6in wide, which is the minimum width to allow free passage through. This means that the two vertical supports (as shown in the illustration on page 38) would make a width of 9in on each side of the door.

Door Flat

It will be noticed that the door flat has no cross timber at the bottom. Instead it should have a steel 'sill' 20mm wide x 5mm thick screwed to the bottom supports. This gives the bottom stability and is thin enough to prevent actors tripping over it as they make an entrance. Professionally made the sill would extend a few inches up the sides of the flat in which case it would be inset to allow the flats to match up with adjoining flats. The double vertical supports to which the door is fixed are reinforced at the bottom with hardboard (as shown in the illustration on page 38).

The door is constructed to fit, and hinged on the appropriate side. A turn-button of wood (or the small metal ones from hardware stores) is usually fixed to keep the door closed. It is better than a ball-catch fastening, as this tends to shake the flat and adjoining flats each time the door is opened or closed. On the rear of the flat on the opposite side to where the door will be hinged, fix two small 15mm thick pieces of wood, door-stops, to prevent the door from swinging right through the flat when it is closed.

If you want to approach perfection, you can equip the door flat with

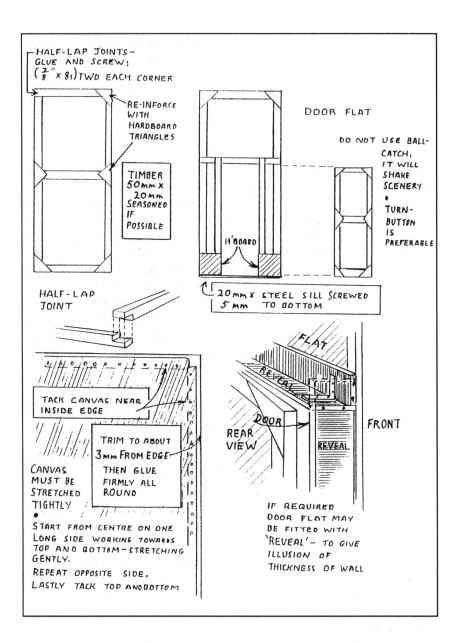

Illustration 4: Flats, how to make them

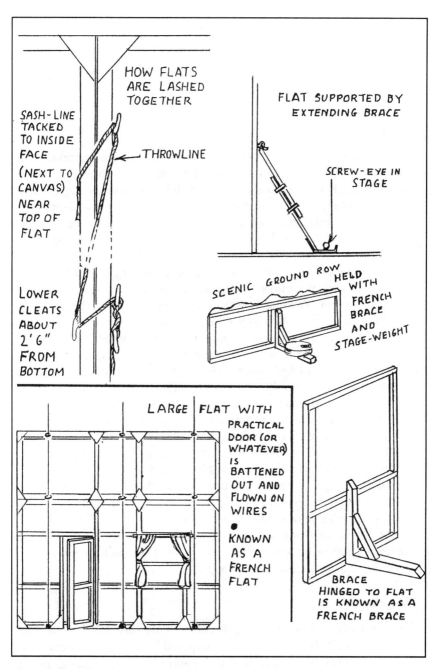

HOW FLATS ARE LASHED TOGETHER

SASH-LINE TACKED TO INSIDE FACE (NEXT TO CANVAS) NEAR TOP OF FLAT

THROWLINE

LOWER CLEATS ABOUT 2'6" FROM BOTTOM

FLAT SUPPORTED BY EXTENDING BRACE

SCREW-EYE IN STAGE

SCENIC GROUND ROW HELD WITH FRENCH BRACE AND STAGE-WEIGHT

LARGE FLAT WITH PRACTICAL DOOR (OR WHATEVER) IS BATTENED OUT AND FLOWN ON WIRES • KNOWN AS A FRENCH FLAT

BRACE HINGED TO FLAT IS KNOWN AS A FRENCH BRACE

Illustration 5: Flats, how to support them

a 'reveal', i.e. two 10cm wide x 15mm thick lengths of wood. The shortest one, the width of the door opening, is fixed across the top, while the other, the height of the door, is laid down the opening side. Fix as shown with brackets to the inner vertical supports. The purpose is to give the illusion of thickness of wall when the door is open.

Canvassing

Canvassing the flats requires care and, if possible, some assistance with the stretching. Lay the frame on the floor, spread the sheeting over it and, starting from the middle of one of the long sides, tack every two inches, working towards the top and bottom, keeping the sheeting or canvas gently stretched. Repeat in this manner the other side (this is where some assistance is helpful), and, lastly, tack the top and bottom.

Tack near the *inside* edge, then trim the canvas to very nearly the edge of the wood – say ⅛in from the edge. If taken right to the edge, or doubled around, the canvas will tend to fray when in use. Then glue firmly all around. You may find that, despite your efforts, the canvas or sheeting will not be as taut as you had hoped. Do not worry unduly as the priming, which comes next, will tighten it up appreciably.

You have a choice of materials for canvassing. Cheapest (and quite acceptable) is unbleached calico sheeting. A little dearer is linen/cotton canvas, which will probably last longer and stand up to handling better. Cotton scenic canvas is robust and professional standard. The prices of course vary according to the amount – it is proportionately cheaper to buy larger quantities. It is advisable to think in terms of over 20m, which is minimal for most jobs. If you need neutral legs and/or borders, Bolton Twill is quite suitable. It comes in two colours: grey and black. Grey is probably the most useful choice in that its neutral colour is less noticeable for a variety of purposes. Black can be a little obtrusive. Cheapest of all is hessian. It can look warm and rich if hung ruched for borders and legs. It does not lend itself well for painting. Gauze (for special effects) is cheap. It comes in two widths: 9ft or 15ft. It can be used to suggest glass in window flats.

Designing sets

The first thing to do in designing a set is to make sure that the proposed set will fulfil all the functions that is required by the anticipated action. To take an obvious example: however beautiful an interior design might be, it will be useless if it doesn't include the window upstage centre, and the dumb waiter door right centre, crucial to the plot.

A set might be (and often is, in smaller drama groups) constructed entirely of flats (examples of this are shown in Chapter 4: Minimal Staging). Or it might include a backcloth, with matching flats or wing-pieces. Whichever way, the sure method of getting it right and avoiding time-wasting mistakes is to make a model first.

Make a model

A few sheets of white card and perhaps some balsa wood lengths from a model shop (if necessary for the construction), sticky tape and a little glue are all the items that are required. *But be sure to make the model to scale*, and set it up on the basic stage ground-plan. *It is also important to make the model in terms of the sizes of cloths and flats that are normally used.*

Draw an outline of the design on the model, perhaps cutting out doors, windows, etc. If you do this, you will see where 'masking' is essential. When you have finalised the preliminary design, check once more that the set is appropriate to the action demanded by the plot.

If a backcloth is to be part of the design, include it in the model and, viewing it from an eye-level appropriate to how it will be seen from the front of the house, check that the perspective of the sketched design is consonant with the flats which will carry the design downstage. When you are satisfied that the model is correct the next thing is to translate the design into the full scale.

The backcloth

When designing the backcloth, work from the drawing you have prepared first. The most important thing to watch is the 'convergence point' or 'vanishing point' – the point at which parallel lines converge. All lines in the design which are parallel should therefore meet at this point. Establishing the precise position of this point can be tricky. You may have to roughly sketch the basis of the design a number of times before you find just the right position (see Illustration 6 on page 42.) There may sometimes be more than one convergence point to cope with. If part of the design shows something on a slope, or angled to show other faces of a building, it may be necessary to work to a second point, even if it is to one side of the design. This is why it is essential to get it right on a drawing first. Mistakes can be expensive and time-consuming to put right on a cloth. Note that lines nearer the spectator

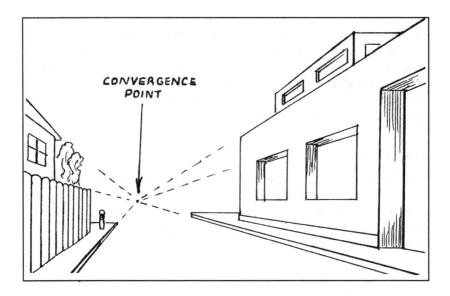

Illustration 6: Scene painting, convergence point
Start design by establishing a convergence point to which lines of perspective will be orientated.

should be thicker and diminish as they approach the vanishing point; failure to adjust lines in this way can ruin an otherwise good design. If you are copying from a picture, perspective will not be so much of a problem, as others will have solved it for you.

To transfer the design or picture to the cloth, lightly pencil vertical and horizontal lines so as to form a squared grid over the design. Now, with the chalk line, reproduce that grid to scale on the cloth. If, for example, you have divided the design into eight squares across and five squares down, then the cloth should be similarly divided eight squares across and five squares down, but proportionately bigger. You should now be able to transfer the design, point by point, from each small square on the picture to the corresponding larger square on the cloth. This will ensure that you get an accurate reproduction of the original design enlarged on the cloth with the correct perspective.

Outlining the picture on the cloth requires care; and some assistance is welcome in holding the ends of the chalk line at the convergence point and the outer edge of the cloth. The small sandbags listed with the tools may also be useful for holding the 6ft straight edge in position when chalking in lines.

Painting Flats

If wing-flats are to be part of the design, they too should be drawn first and orientated to the general perspective, using the same chalk-line techniques. Outline the flats on the floor, then they can be propped against a wall for painting. Having got the outline and perspective right, it is then a matter of choosing the colours. Once again it is best to try out the general scheme on the model.

Ready-mixed emulsion paints may be used. Alternatively achieve the colour you want, in the professional way, by mixing whiting and size (as for priming), together with dry colours in powder form. Colours may be obtained from scenic material suppliers (see list of suppliers on page 168).

If the cloths and flats envisaged are largely confined to depicting domestic interiors, the range of colours required may not be all that extensive, unless there are windows showing gardens, or if there are outdoor scenes when a range of colours would be desirable. Nature offers a very wide range of shades as you will discover if you look critically at some outdoor vista. (An artists's tip: look at a view under your arm, and with inverted head survey the scene. You will be surprised at the variety of colours you perceive which were not so apparent from a normal position.)

Here is a list of colours which can be used and blended for many purposes:

Dark Ultramarine	Brunswick Green (Dark)
Light Blue	Venetian Red
Chrome	Crimson Lake
Yellow Ochre	Pink
Burnt Sienna	Black
Brunswick Green (Light)	

Remember to paint in artificial light – similar to that on stage. Do not attempt to paint in fluorescent tube lighting. It plays havoc with colours. A 1kw floodlight is suitable, and two if large areas are concerned. Test colours on white paper first, and allow to dry. Colours will dry to a paler shade. If you have a large area to cover, say a backcloth and perhaps matching flats, mix enough colour to do the whole as you might have difficulty in mixing a second batch of colour to exactly match the first.

Painting backcloths

The bottom of the cloth should be sandwiched between two battens, the outside edges of which should be chamfered and smoothed (to prevent damage to the cloth when it is rolled). The battens are then firmly nailed together. After the top has been battened, it is then hung ready for priming.

It is unlikely that the amateur will have the luxury of a paint-frame. An alternative method is possible. Hang the cloth as usual from the top batten, then pick up the bottom batten with the set of lines immediately behind, so that the cloth is suspended top and bottom. Now put a length of metal tubing (conduit piping) to rest in the bottom of the fold. You can then lower the cloth to a comfortable height and start the painting from the top, raising the top batten and lowering the bottom batten (behind) as you progress.

Another method, if there is no way of hanging the cloth to work on, is to lay the cloth on the floor. If it is on the stage, it is wise to lay down old newspapers first to prevent colours from seeping through and staining the stage. If the cloth has been well sized, however, this should not be a big problem.

For both cloths and flats, fill in the large areas of colour first, then add outlines and details when dry. The colours should dry fairly quickly. Be bold and impressionistic. Think in terms of poster design rather than oil paintings. Fine detail will merge and be lost from the front. The aim is representation rather than reality.

Tools for painting

You will need a few simple tools for priming and painting flats and cloths:

A 3ft rigid rule, or a three-fold carpenter's rule. A retractable metal tape rule is also useful.

A 6ft straight edge for drawing long lines. Do check that it really is straight. (You may find it helpful to mark it off into foot lengths.)

A chalk line: this is a length of thin string, which is rubbed with charcoal or chalk, and held taut at both ends in the required position. The centre is then picked up and 'pinged' against the canvas, leaving a thin line of chalk. It is a most convenient way of marking long lines on a cloth.

Charcoal drawing sticks and/or coloured chalk for marking designs.

Charcoal brushes off easily.

A 3ft bamboo cane or dowelling. Fasten the charcoal stick or chalk firmly at one end with elastic bands. This will allow you to stand away from the cloth when drawing the design.

A couple of buckets in which to mix quantities of size or colour.

A pot for boiling size and a brush for applying.

A collection of jampots to contain colours.

A supply of white paper (a shelf-roll would be fine) for trying out colours.

A supply of rags for mopping up.

Two smallish clean sandbags might be of assistance in holding the straight edge when using it to draw lines.

Brushes

A 4in brush for laying in large areas
A 2in and a 1in for smaller areas.
For details: 'Fitches' sizes 3 and 6.

Always clean a brush immediately after use. If you let it harden it will deteriorate, be a nuisance to clean when you next start, and its useful life will be shortened.

Priming

A good working quantities formula is 8lb (3.6kg) whiting to ½lb (0.225kg) concentrated size, mixed with boiling water, in the quantity as advised by the size manufacturer. The solution should not be too thick. Using a 4in brush, apply evenly and allow to dry thoroughly. It will tighten to a firm surface ready for painting.

Aniline dye cloths

There are some cloths made not to be battened out but folded and stored in baskets. These are aniline dye cloths. They come with webbing and ties on top ready to be tied to a batten. Sometimes they will have a chain sewn in the bottom to make them hang straight. Gauzes are usually painted with aniline dyes.

The dyes come in fine powder form or in cakes. Make a solution in fairly hot water, then when fully dissolved, stir into a larger container of warm water, adding a little at a time, until the right shade is achieved. As before, test the shade on paper before applying to the cloth. It will dry a paler shade.

A little more care is required in the making of these cloths since it is impossible to paint over. A stray brush mark or splash is there to stay and you cannot correct a mistaken line. Accuracy of brushwork is therefore essential. The best advice is to experiment on a spare length of cloth until you get the 'feel' of the material before starting on the real thing. Aniline dye cloths give a very bright colour effect, generally more brilliant than pigments.

Overall design

A well-designed production will imply close co-operation between Director, Scenic Designer and Wardrobe Designer (if costumes are being made especially for it – if they are being hired, enquiries may be made to the costumiers about predominating colours so that harmony with the scenery may be achieved). If there is a Lighting Designer he too could sit in on the preliminary consultation, when he might make useful notes about choice of colours. He might at least avoid mistakes. A beautiful blue velvet will look like mud if exposed to red light! If there is a person in charge of printed publicity, he or she might well be kept informed, since a predominant colour scheme might be extended to posters, cards, handbills and programmes.

Fire-proofing

Fire-proofing is obligatory. A visiting fire-chief has the power to refuse permission for a performance to take place, or to stop it at any time if he is not satisfied that the items of scenic environment are adequately fire-proof. Cloths, flats, costumes and vulnerable props should all be fire-proofed.

FOR SCENERY: 1lb (0.45kg) phosphate of ammonia and 2lb (0.91kg) chloride of ammonia in 1½ gall (6.8 litres) of water. Brush or spray on. Should be effective for about six months.

FOR LIGHTER FABRICS: 10oz (283g) of borax and 8oz (227g) of boric acid to 1 gall (4.5 litres) of water. Dip fabrics into the solution.

4 | *Minimal Staging*

The open stage and DIY scenic units

Mounting a theatrical production can be an expensive business. The facility with which film and television maintain attention to the screen by constant, and instant, scene changes puts the stage production, in this respect, at a disadvantage. Such practical and economic-based limitations, however, have led to an increased awareness of the theatre's two great strengths. First, the advantage of the incomparable immediacy of the live performance; and second, its ability to concentrate on the message without the spectator being distracted by the medium.

The interposition of all the paraphernalia of film and television technology between the dramatist, artiste and the spectator can introduce an element of artificiality to the freshness of the performance be it song, poem or play. Consequently there has been a reawakening to the very essence of theatre: the art of the actor and the dramatist, as it emerged in the early theatre of the Greeks and of Shakespeare.

These remarks are not intended in any way to denigrate film, television or the special skills of acting for the camera, which are art forms in their own right. These are separate subjects. We are concerned here with the live theatre. And a most important ingredient of the live theatre is the element of make-believe inherent in the stage performance. It is precisely this that pinpoints the essential difference between screen and stage. The screen may swamp the message with too much peripheral realism. The stage – in whatever form – retains the vital element of make-believe. It is just this element that has given a new impetus to dramatic art in the way of experimental theatre: historic plays in modern dress; minimal staging and open stage production where dramatist and actor present the 'message' of the play with little or no scenery.

Of course there remains a place and a need for intricate staging, lavish costumes and spectacular effects, the immediate impact of which so enhances the particular pleasure of one kind of theatre-going. This aspect is dealt with later in Part Two, when the staging of modern musicals is considered. Here, the concern is with the techniques by which theatre lovers (which all amateur drama groups must be) can practise their art in ways within the means of moderately-sized amateur groups.

The first requirement of the performing artiste is that he must be seen. Therefore, in most cases, it follows that either he must be raised up so he can be visible to all, or he will remain on the floor and the audience must be raised. The first alternative leads to the traditional proscenium stage, while the second is most likely to lead to the 'open stage' (or thrust stage) and 'theatre-in-the-round' productions. This style makes use of the simplest scenic effects, and will be considered first.

Theatre-in-the-round productions

In some instances, the acting area will be a space with the audience seated in tiers on all four sides. The actors will therefore make their entrances and exits via the aisles between the seating. In this situation any scenic effects must be minimal, since anything bulky or high will obstruct the view of some section of the spectators. The most effective means of achieving dramatic effect open to the Director lies, first, in selective lighting and, second, in the use of rostra. A number of rostra pre-set at strategic positions and arranged at different heights, with attendant treads, will break the monotony of a plain floor, lending variety and an architectural framework; this may be exploited by placing the action of various scenes at different positions, possibly bounding a larger central space. In this kind of presentation there is likely to be more usable acting space than offered by the traditional proscenium stage. The minimum amount of furniture or props required for sub-plot scenes can be pre-set before the performance at the designated positions, leaving the central area for big scenes.

There are no house-tabs, runners or drop-cloths to mark the beginning and ending of scenes. Instead it is done with lighting. At the finish of one scene, the lights black out, the actors quickly take their positions at the appropriate scene-area and the lights go up on that particular part of the set. In bringing into existence from the darkness now this scene, now that, together with the intimacy, the nearness of the actors to the spectators, the power of carefully controlled lighting to create the ambience of dreams, is most dramatically potent. Yet because the action takes place, as it were, amongst them, the spectators experience the dream-like quality, while at the same time having the feeling (as we say of a vivid dream) of it being 'like real life.'

With little scenic environment to add colour to productions, costumes will assume a greater importance. This is part of the reason why theatre-in-the-round may be more suited to historic or pageant-type productions. Spectacle will be based on colourful costumes and carefully composed groupings, using the larger acting areas and different levels to achieve interesting effects. It is doubtful if intimate plays such as Oscar Wilde's *The Importance of Being Earnest* or Noel Coward's *Private Lives* would be so successful without the period settings within a proscenium arch.

Some plays of an indeterminate period or location, e.g. *Waiting for Godot*, or those having political, social or spiritual connotations, may lend themselves to the impressionistic, simplistic, scenic style of the open stage even when played on the proscenium stage. Here again, selective lighting will play an important part.

Open stage productions

In some instances the acting area will be set against a wall, with the seating on three sides. In this event, while much of the foregoing still applies, there may be, as well as rostra, opportunity for minimal scenic effects.

The most useful of these would be the introduction of a blue sky-cloth, lit from beneath with a magazine ground trough and from above by a magazine batten. Variously illuminated, the cloth will create the effect of open air, daylight, evening or night. The right colour circuits will also give the appearance of indoor backing to, say, an historic hall, castle or cathedral. The atmosphere of the play's location or period can be suggested by the addition of a few simple pieces, such as columns, an arch piece, or a low scenic ground row set close to the backdrop. If the dressing-rooms lead from the backing wall, a backcloth set a couple of feet or so from the wall will afford players the opportunity to cross behind unseen, so as to make entrances from whichever side required, as well as serving to mask entrances and exits to the dressing-rooms.

To achieve the control desirable, lighting for open stage presentations of the kind discussed will (other than the possibility of magazine battens to illuminate a backcloth) almost certainly consist of a mixture of Fresnel Spotlights, with variable beam-spread, and Profile Spots. A control panel with at least one preset is eminently desirable, as is the positioning of the control panel and operator somewhere in the auditorium, where he has a clear view of the whole acting area. With scenic requirements making less demands on the budget, it is well worth investing in lighting facilities and controls wherever possible. Lighting is your chief ally.

Simple staging

Open stage or theatre-in-the-round require a purpose-built hall or one that can be adapted with tiered seating. It is probable that the majority of amateur drama groups, however, will perform on the traditional proscenium stage. It is also likely that the stage will be equipped with at least a pair of running curtains to serve as house-tabs, some side-curtains and a curtain at the back of the stage.

Many books on amateur staging repeat the advice that simple staging should start with curtain sets. Ideas are suggested, such as parting the back-curtain to indicate a door or adding a flat with a window either painted on or cut out. Small scenic ground rows, a self-standing tree or a lamp-post representing a park or a street are suggested. This advice may well suit groups whose interest in theatrical production is of a sporadic and elementary nature. For those societies who take the business of production more seriously, the advice to start with curtain sets may not be to their long-term advantage. There will come a time when the keen society will want something a little more ambitious than playing in grey-curtained sets. They will become aware that such settings, however bolstered with necessary furniture, fail to convey to the spectator in any convincing way, that he is looking at, say, Lord Marmaduke's penthouse in Park Lane. Or that the same grey curtains with a tree to one side have now become Hyde Park.

A set of running curtains will serve as house-tabs. Instead of using curtains for settings, or if the stage is being equipped from scratch dressing overall with curtains, the alternative offered here is to invest in scenic canvas and timber to make your own flats. The word 'invest' is deliberately chosen, for what is proposed is a scheme for a set of multi-purpose scenic items capable of being used repeatedly in any number of settings. An added advantage lies in being able to present fresh, new, colourful settings for each production. This advantage should be taken into account when working out the initial outlay. It should be borne in mind that such costs would be spread out over many succeeding productions.

Multi-purpose scenic units

The scheme proposed requires fourteen basic pieces, which are made up from eight basic flats, four arch flats, a door flat and a window flat (plus two french window transformation pieces as and if required). The eight basic flats are hinged to compose four book-wings. The four arch flats are hinged to make two arch book-wings. Together with the door and window flats, this makes up eight units in all.

Here's how to go about it:

1 Four book-wings

Study the instructions and illustrations in Making Flats (see page 36). Make eight flats. The dimensions recommended are 10ft high x 4ft wide (though this will depend on the size of your stage). When completed, hinge them in pairs using three double-fold screen hinges for each pair. These will allow the flats to be opened either towards the front or towards the back and so achieve a greater degree of flexibility in use.

2 Door flat

Make a door flat, as shown in Making Flats (see page 36). Now study Illustration 7 on page 52 which shows how to construct the next items.

3 Arch flats

Arch flats are simply the framework of the simple flat without the bottom and centre cross-members. For stability, the bottoms are reinforced with steel 'sills' (as described for the door flats). An arch is made from half of a sheet of 8ft x 4ft hardboard. Thus you get four arch pieces from two sheets. Take each half-sheet and at the sawn edge mark the centre, i.e. 2ft from each side. From the centre, draw a half-circle with a radius of 20½ins. Carefully cut out the half-circle and you will be left with the arch piece, with a 3½in 'shoulder' on each side. Nail the hardboard (rough side to the front – as it takes paint better) to the top of the framework. Copper hardboard nails will not rust. Make four arch flats and hinge them in pairs to make two book-wing arch flats, again using double-fold screen hinges.

4 Window flat

As will be seen in the illustration on page 52 this is the basic flat unit with a hardboard top and bottom and a gap between. To show the construction, the sketch depicts the rear side of the flat, but the hardboard and 1in laths to make the window across the gap must be nailed to the *front* of the flat. The bottom of the window opening should be approximately 2ft 6in from the bottom of the flat and allow

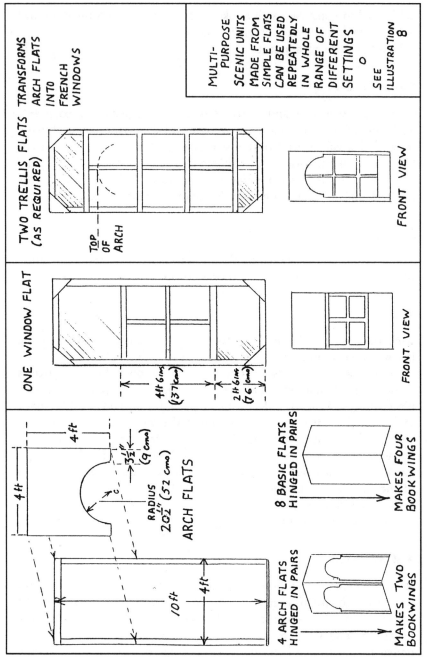

Illustration 7: Multi-purpose scenic units, construction

an opening of approximately 4ft 6in for the height of the window.

5 French window conversion

These pieces may be left until required. An outline flat (i.e. without the canvas) with 1in laths nailed as shown, is made up. This, if bolted to the rear of an arch flat (but with laths towards the front) will transform it into a French window. (3in x ¼in bolts with wing nuts will enable it to be quickly fixed.) A pair of arch flats with these pieces added will be very useful for country house scenes. The arches can be used singly, by unscrewing one side of the hinges.

Door flats, window flats and single arch flats should be braced from behind. A book-wing opened out to form a straight run must also be braced. In Illustration 8 on page 54, four examples of settings made with the units described are shown. A little thought and ingenuity will enable any number of combinations to be made up. The settings shown are basic designs. Ancillary pieces and dressings are added as required. In the two exterior sets, a scenic ground-row and a free-standing tree have been added. The cubes shown are made from tea-chests, with a covering of unbleached calico firmly glued on and painted a light grey to resemble stone. In the interior sets, a little furniture has been sketched in and the window flats are shown with curtains added.

Note that in drawings 1 and 3 the book-wing pairs (B2 and B3) have been used as backing pieces. In drawing 3 the single arch piece showing on the right is one half of a hinged pair, supported by the other half of the pair out of sight behind book-wing B4.

This scheme was actually used as the basis for a long-season summer production. All the flats, borders and a false proscenium were white in order to reflect a variety of colour schemes, obtained with lighting. This was a specialised use. For a drama society, the flats may be painted as appropriate to each production.

Backing

As a backing to this scheme, a blue sky-cloth is the perfect accompaniment. Preferably lit from a lighting ground trough from below and a magazine batten (cyclorama batten) from above, it can convey the space of outdoors, or back an interior with windows upstage. Where possible, the back wall of the stage, if of even texture, could be painted a light blue to provide a backing – but check that there is a way for players to cross the stage to make entrances.

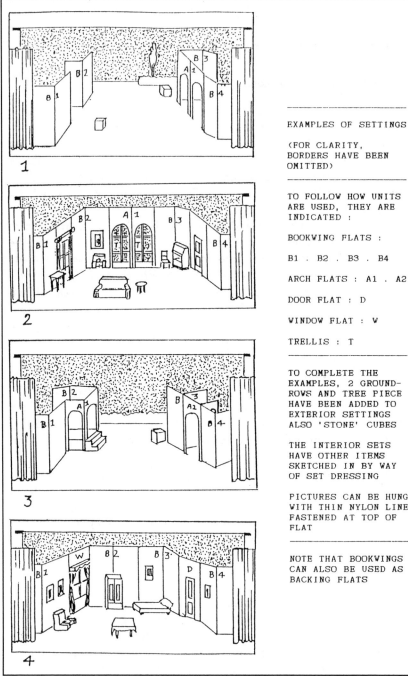

Illustration 8: Multi-purpose scenic units, example.

Concert or musical show

The four book-wings set in pairs, one behind the other, each side of the stage, will make smart wings. The arch flats can also be used as a decorative background.

Borders

Of course borders will be required to mask tops of flats and lighting bars. These can be of some light-proof material (e.g. Grey Bolton Twill, from scenic material suppliers) hung in ruches. A pleasing refinement would be to make straight-edged borders from the same sheeting as used for the flats and tie them to the same bar as the light-proof borders, but hang them in front. These could be painted to match the colours as used for the flats for any particular show.

5 | Lighting

Theory and gear

Basic Theory

In the view of many of those who work in the theatre, of all the technical aspects of stagecraft the one that ranks highest in importance is lighting. Why is this?

Most dramatic performances (but not all) are representations of reality. Implicit in dramatic representation is the element of make-believe. The dramatist, the actors and the technicians ask the spectator to accept, temporarily, the artificial reality they create for him; in other words, he is required to suspend his disbelief. They combine to create a vision, a dream of what might be. Inevitably, therefore, there must be, in creating that 'reality', the element of enchantment. And in no respect is enchantment more readily accessible than through the use of light and darkness. Students of drama will recognise that what we are discussing here is the first canon of dramatic art.

Suspension of disbelief

Consider the dream. In dreams people and events appear from and disappear into the darkness of oblivion. As they arise they will carry the dreamer along with the conviction of reality. Disbelief comes on awakening, but while the dream persists, however irrational or unreal, the spectator – the dreamer – accepts the reality of the experience because in that state he is enchanted. Dreams arise from, and are surrounded by, the darkness of sleep. In darkness itself lies a residual primeval fear – an uneasiness, an expectation of the unexpected, a feeling that something may happen at any moment. In this brief exposition, is it not clear that in the theatre, by the use of darkness and light, we have all the ingredients to parallel the experience of the dream?

Whether the actors have costumes or not, whether they are surrounded by scenery or not, in a darkened space, where the darkness itself creates an atmosphere of tension and expectancy, skilful use of selective lighting, making people and events appear from and vanish into the darkness, captures the attention of the spectator. The Director can create the ambience, the enchantment of the dream – but only if he has control over these elements. To what extent does he possess that control?

The history of stage lighting is a history of the development of that essential control. At present it has reached a very high standard indeed. A great many drama groups or societies attached to schools or colleges are likely to perform on stages equipped by professional stage lighting firms, and will from the inception have absorbed, almost unconsciously, the importance of lighting and its control. Societies who hire professional theatres, will generally have the benefit of up-to-date equipment. Other less fortunate groups who perform in circumstances maintained entirely by their own resources, and wishing to develop, might do a lot worse than explore the opportunities inherent in good lighting control.

However, the powerful impact of modern lighting may be abused. Bemused by the technical facilities offered by the medium, television directors, by an over-use of camera tricks, and frequent or gratuitously unnatural camera angles, sometimes commit the sin of obscuring the message by an excess of form. In a similar manner, Lighting Designers dazzled by technical possibilities may sometimes emphasise the lighting to an extent that diminishes the performance it is intended to enhance. For example, impressive scenery, beautiful costumes and talented performers, can be upstaged all too easily by a row of lights high up backstage, winking on and off or enveloped in seemingly ubiquitous smoke, not only plainly visible but dazzling the eyes of spectators in the stalls.

However, complex multiplicity of lanterns such as is favoured by professional Lighting Designers may not be feasible for the amateur society, who may often have to use less up-to-date installations – not infrequently ordinary lamp bulbs in biscuit tins!

Tools of the trade

The tools of the Lighting Designer fall into two categories: the lanterns, instruments or, in the latest phrase, 'luminaires' (a term adopted because of its international recognition); and the controls. A consideration of both categories may be useful.

Lanterns

The range of lanterns available now is enormous and there is not enough space to describe them all (Strand Lighting list over thirty types in their catalogue and continue to extend the range). They are, however, developments of a few basic types, so a brief survey of them is possible.

MAGAZINE BATTENS are rows of lamps, each in a separate reflector housing, so that they can accommodate colour filters, either all the same, or so arranged that different circuits will activate a repeated pattern of colours along the length of each batten. Some are sectionalised allowing centre or other portions to be activated, thus providing a degree of flexibility. Once standard equipment in most theatres, they have been superseded in many modern installations by individual lanterns. This is to be regretted since they remain very useful for a 'light-spread' or 'colour-wash' over large areas, particularly for light entertainment, musicals or pantomimes.

FOOTLIGHTS (or 'FLOATS'), a name derived from their original source, when wicks in little supports floated in a trough of oil) are equivalent to the magazine battens, but set at the front edge of the stage at foot level – hence 'footlights'. Also absent from more modern stages, like the overhead magazine battens, they can, when used with discretion, be extremely useful for 'filling-in'. They are very helpful and glamorous in variety shows.

GROUND TROUGHS are like footlights, but are usually on a mobile mount to facilitate quick positioning at the bottom of cycloramas, cloths or drapes from where they throw light upwards.

SPOTLIGHTS can roughly be divided into two types: the Profile, which gives a sharp-edged pool of light; and the Fresnel, with its special contoured lens giving a softer-edged pool of light and therefore more suitable for blending its area of coverage with others. Usually adjustable, both come in a range of sizes, shapes, variation of throw and angle of spread. There are bifocal spotlights with facilities to give a hard-edged or a soft-edged light pattern, and Strand Lighting have developed a lantern, Prelude PC (Prism Convex), which manages to incorporate the qualities of both Profile and Fresnel.

ACTING AREAS still exist in many theatres. Usually hung directly above, they are mostly used as basic lighting lanterns.

FLOODS, as the name implies, give a very wide angle flood of light. They are useful for lighting cycloramas and, with discretion, as 'applause pullers' in variety shows.

FOLLOW-SPOTS are intensely bright lanterns with systems of mirrors and lenses to enable an adjustable beam of light to be thrown from the back of the theatre to the stage. Up-to-date models are equipped with colour-filter magazines and adjustable shutters so that the light thrown on stage can appear shaped like a square, or letter-box, or just a slit. A very useful lantern which used intelligently and thoughtfully can convey a great deal of the Director's concept of the production as well as contributing 'glamour'.

MOVING EFFECTS: again a large range from moving clouds, rain and snow, to fire, sea, or dazzling colour effects. There are also static effects such as colour patterns and rainbows. All these require a very great deal of thought and care if they are to be used effectively. Used badly, they can result in absurdity.

PROJECTORS are lanterns which, with different lens systems (long, medium or wide angle), can be used to project commercial-size slides as parts of a background. There are also specially developed high-power projectors for projecting scenery. These also require much thought and care in their use, since the rest of the stage lighting has to be tailored and adjusted to render an effective whole. Usually, specially made perspective-adjusted slides are required.

LINNEBACH LANTERNS are a simple means of projecting impressionistic or abstract patterns on to backcloths. They can be made up on the spot, requiring a point-light source, no lens, and often a large 16in x 16in slide of glass with the design painted on with transparent glass paint. It is possible to create designs using stuck-on shapes cut from colour filters and opaque black paint. (A Fresnel spotlight with lens temporarily removed and some arrangement to hold the glass slide in front – perhaps with the co-operation of a metalworker to rig a fitment on to a stand – will serve the purpose.)

MANOUVERABLE SPOTLIGHTS designed for television studios are available. These allow beam-spread, angle and light position to be remotely-controlled, so they can be adjusted without the use of ladders.

COLOUR CHANGE LANTERNS have remote-control random colour change, or are the more familiar revolving colour-wheel lanterns.

COLOURS: different colour effects are obtained by the use of colour filters. They are usually referred to as 'gels' because they were originally made of coloured gelatine. This has now been replaced by a more durable material. The range of colour shades now available is extensive enough to cater for the most fastidious colour requirements. Colour swatch books are available to assist experiment and choice. When choosing shades of colour, a more effective way than looking at a light through them is to judge their shade by making a card mask. Cut a slit in a piece of card a little smaller than the swatch and look at the colour cast when a light is shone through the slit with colour sample in front.

GOBOS are metal masks with circles, squares or other abstract shapes cut in. Slid into Profile spotlights they project the shapes on to backdrops, etc. For short-time use, you can improvise by using the very thin aluminium pie or cake dishes (the throwaway kind used for freezing or cooking), flattened and cut to desired size and pattern.

LIGHT PATTERNS: the author has obtained some pleasing effects by using a combination of colour filters and offcuts of patterned glass cut by a helpful glazier into 3¾in x 3¾in slides to fit commercial projectors fitted with wide-angle lenses.

Slides to fit projectors are not difficult to make. A piece of thin plain glass 3¾in x 3¾in can have the design painted on using transparent paints, the kind made for painting on glass, obtained from good art shops – or even shapes cut from Cinemoid, or spotlight colour filters stuck on. Cover with a second piece of thin plain glass and bind the edge with passe-partout. If there is space to project from behind a translucent cloth, there is little difficulty, but if projected from the side, there will be problems of perspective to overcome. It is better to attempt abstract designs.

LIGHT ANGLES. Spotlights are often set on stage bars to project across the stage, so that a spotlight on the O/P side of centre might be directed to the P/S. This is thought to add contour to the actors' faces. It also gives a wider spread of light when lighting facilities are limited. However, like most other rules, it is not invariable. Added intensity can be obtained by directing the throw straight on – useful for front-of-house focussing.

BARNDOORS are used to contain the light-spread of spotlights. A fitment is slid into the front of the lantern, carrying four metal 'doors' or flaps which may be adjusted to mask the light as desired.

EFFECTS such as flash boxes, maroons, smoke, fog and snow machines are available. They can be bought, or hired on a weekly basis from theatrical lighting firms.

Controls

PATCH PANEL is an electrical panel backstage which allows various stage lights to be plugged in, perhaps temporarily, so as to be controlled by dimmer circuits.

CIRCUITS and CHANNELS are terms with similar meaning. A circuit is the route of the mains electricity supply to one or more lanterns. When a dimmer control is introduced in that circuit, it has become the practice to refer to the modified circuit as a 'channel'.

CONTROL PANELS. There was a time when somewhere high up on a gantry on the P/S of the stage there would be an enormous array of wheels, screw-in handles, levers and switches. Looking rather like the driving cab of an immense traction engine, it was the 'board' controlling the dimmers and the stage lighting. Thanks to electronics, that 'board' has been reduced to a comparatively small panel of fingertip controls, now usually set somewhere front of house, where the operator has a clear view of the stage. Control panels come in a range of sizes from 6 manual faders to colossal 999 channel systems.

PRESETS (when used in a lighting context as distinct from stage presets). A preset is a lighting cue consisting of one or more lanterns, perhaps balanced at different levels of luminosity, set beforehand ready to come into operation when a master switch is activated. It could be the first lighting cue ready at the start of the performance, or the next cue set up while the preceding one is operative. The preset is the very essence of smooth lighting practice, offering artistic opportunities to Director, Designer and panel operator alike.

MANUAL PRESET PANELS have a number of dimmer channels responsive to fingertip controls, with levels of luminosity indicated. The required lanterns, connected to the designated main circuit, are channelled through numbered sliding controls at chosen levels of dimming. In this state of readiness they wait until the master control is operated in timed build, fade, or snap-up. The disposition and number of lamps in use and their levels of luminosity are referred to as the cue 'state'. The initial cue 'state' can be modified at any time, by adding or subtracting the sliding controls.

A simple preset panel will have a duplicate set of sliding controls alongside and while one cue, e.g. cue 15, is in operation, the next cue, 16, can be set up ready to supersede the previous cue by operating the master controls, so effecting a smooth change from one cue 'state' to the next. After the change-over is made, cue 17 is set up on the first panel, ready to come into operation. In this way, each cue is set up manually, according to the lighting plot, as the performance continues. Sometimes if the plot is complicated, with quick changes, some assistance may be required to set succeeding cue 'states'. There are panels with three or more manual presets available.

MEMORY CONTROL PANELS. A quantum leap in the control of lighting occurred when Strand Lighting came up with the memory panel. This, as may be inferred, is a computer-related system for storing the cue 'states' in a memory. This means that all the cue 'states' can be set up during the lighting rehearsal and faithfully reproduced in proper succession in obedience to the timed operation of the master controls. In this way, while the cue 'state' remains constant, the timing of the cue-change remains under the control of the operator. The memory panel allows any cue 'state' to be modified at any time. It also obviates mistakes due to an operator's lapses in setting up the dimmer slider patterns during the performance.

These memory panels which offer so much are by no means beyond the financial scope of the moderately successful amateur society. They offer the last word in accurate control. There are control panels with additional refinements to do with the handling of a multiplicity of channels and effects, but enough has been written to answer the question posed about the Director's control over lighting. The technology presently available would appear adequate to support any of the Lighting Designer's imaginative demands. How the Director sets about using the lighting systems and control will be covered in Part Two (see Chapter 12, Lighting Design).

Where to start

It is scarcely possible to offer advice on details of a lighting installation suitable for an amateur group without knowing the size of the stage, the kind of performances contemplated, the geography of the hall and the financial circumstances. Very broadly, for a society contemplating a programme of mixed presentations, including plays, occasional musical entertainments, pantomimes, etc., the following may offer a guide.

Some Fresnel wide beam-spread lanterns set in the auditorium and directed at the stage – sufficient in number to cover the front of the stage. This should be regarded as basic lighting. (The number will depend upon where the lanterns are placed, the distance of throw and the angle of beam-spread appropriate to the lantern pattern.) On stage, in the No 1 bar position, a minimum of three wide-angle Fresnels on each side, to act as basic lighting to cover the area upstage, where the front-of-house lanterns do not adequately reach. Further back, say mid-stage, is where, when financial considerations are important, a sectionalised magazine batten can be very useful in providing a basic light-spread (or colour-wash). Otherwise, mid-stage, another six Fresnels. It would be useful to add, say, six pattern 123s (smaller Fresnels) to achieve a minimum of selective lighting possibility – sometimes as side lighting.

Next, there should be a mobile ground trough to light the backdrop and a magazine batten to illuminate it from above. A blue sky-cloth so lit can be immensely useful. Most important is a control panel with at least one preset. After this bare set-up, the addition of a couple of Profile spots, a couple of colour-change spots from the front and a follow-spot would make welcome additions to a variety of presentations, including concerts, variety shows and musicals.

If the Director or Lighting Designer is fortunate enough to have a plentiful stock of lanterns at his disposal he may be able to light the production in the manner of the specialist. This involves dividing the stage into approximately 6ft squares and then focussing a pair of spotlights, set apart from each other, so as to make an angle of throw of about 45 degrees. The spotlights are then fitted with filters of different degrees of 'warmth' or 'coolness' or 'dominant'/'secondary' colours, so as to achieve a modelling or contour effect on the actor.

Lighting in this manner calls for a multiplicity of lanterns to cover the areas for each scene setting and it will become more complex if the play calls for a diversity of effects, e.g. an interior, a sunny exterior and perhaps moonlight. A different pair of spotlights may then be necessary for each of the 6ft segments that go to make up the area for each scene.

This is venturing into the area of specialised lighting design and perhaps beyond the resources of time and equipment for the average amateur group. For more fortunate organisations who aspire to this standard, Strand Lighting have a teaching pack on offer with much useful information on planning, rigging and plotting the lighting. Their publication *Strandbook* is both a catalogue and a source of much useful information on planning and lighting (see list of suppliers on page 167).

6 | Sound

Amplification, taping and cueing effects

Microphones on stage

Sound is sometimes a contentious issue in theatres. Older theatres with circles that wrapped around to each side of the stage, horseshoe fashion, were acoustically efficient, and amplification was largely unnecessary. Unfortunately, newer designed theatres and 'all-purpose' halls often lack such acoustic viability. Also people have been so conditioned to amplification, both of music and the human voice, that they come to expect it, and think there is something wrong if it isn't there. Performers too have come to rely on amplification, and almost universally use it to excess. Ideally the sound control operator should have his control panel somewhere in the auditorium so he can hear what the audience hears. There should also be monitor speakers fixed backstage by the proscenium arch, so the performers have some indication of the volume, otherwise they will be likely to complain that they cannot be heard.

If microphones across the floats position and suspended microphones are used, a control panel and operator will be imperative since the configuration and proximity of scenic items in various scenes will affect the sound balance. A cloth let in near a suspended microphone can easily set up an unwelcome noise. The position of the performers in relation to the foot-microphones will also make monitoring necessary.

Hand-held microphones, while providing stylistic flair to some solo performers and desperate support to others, are grotesquely out of place in musical plays. Unobtrusive radio microphones bring their own crop of troubles; for instance, extreme vigilance should be exercised in switching them off every time the character leaves the stage. Unless all characters are provided with radio microphones there may be the matter of balance between those who are 'miked-up' and those who are not. Their use can be expensive. Good ones can cost up to £2,000 and there is also the cost of the licence issued under the Wireless and Telegraphy Act, administered by the Department of Trade and Industry. Equipment has to be passed by government inspectors to check that they will be used within the allowed frequencies. Unchecked microphones are illegal and, if used, there is the possibility of interference with emergency services. A message from the police, the fire brigade, the ambulance service or taxi firms unexpectedly interpolated into a performance is guaranteed to reduce the most earnest, artistic endeavours to hilarious shambles. Legally, too, it is the individual user who is liable to prosecution and confiscation of the offending equipment.

Some reinforcement of choral numbers by the use of pre-recorded tapes is possible and useful in certain situations, especially where choreographic effects are prominent. However, they require great care in pre-recording and rehearsal – especially when rehearsing with full orchestra, where the Music Director will require headphones, tuned to the special 'cued-in' tape. Almost certainly extra rehearsal time will be necessary, and this can be expensive if the musicians are in receipt of rehearsal pay. There are also legal copyright requirements and fees in connection with the Performing Rights Society; and the Phonographic and Mechanical Reproduction Societies have to be considered.

Altogether amplification and sound reinforcement is a specialist area and, at least to begin with, it is advisable to call on the services of the expert in the field. His advice may obviate many costly blunders and wasted money. There are specialist firms who offer services and equipment hire. There is likely to be a local public address/radio firm with its own expert; if so, it may be feasible to let him install what is required. If repeated for other productions, he may consider a reduced charge – especially if an advertisement of his services, plus a programme credit, is offered.

Sound effects

Few theatres now possess wind machines, wooden thunder troughs, rain machines or their like, though they may still have an iron thunder sheet hanging in some obscure corner. There may also be a door knocker or door slam, but the availability of recorded sound effects nowadays usually results in the use of the tape-deck.

French's and EMI have a range of recorded effects for hire, and the BBC has published a splendid collection of effects on record, with descriptions on the sleeve and indications of track and duration on the record. These may be reproduced direct from the record, though for precise control and cueing it is infinitely preferable to transfer the desired effect on to a reel-to-reel tape–machine. When the effect is on tape it can be more easily manipulated.

There may arise occasions when the sound effect is required to last longer than is available on the record. With the use of a second tape recorder and careful editing to ensure a join where it will not be detected, a tape loop can be made. This can be used to prolong the effect indefinitely. If the suitable place for a join involves many feet of tape, the resultant loop may be unwieldy. However, a clean glass bottle (preferably weighted with water inside) set at the required distance from the machine will make a satisfactory extended temporary capstan. With the loop on one machine, record it back on to the tape on the first machine for a longer duration than is likely to be required, so that the sound operator has a little leeway to fade in and fade out at the appointed cue. If the tape-deck has facilities for transferring from track to track (such as the Revox), effects can be blended and superimposed. Wherever an effect is to be used, ensure there is a recording long enough to match any variation in spread or pace of the action on stage.

Cueing

Revolution counters on tape-machines can be unreliable. For precise cueing it is better to mark the tape itself with narrow adhesive labels, such as can be obtained from most stationers. They measure 3½cm x 5mm and are narrow enough to fit inside the width of the tape. There is room to put cue numbers and titles on each label.

Separate each effect with two or three feet of blank tape and, when all the effects have been edited in sequence, you will probably have a tape with many joins. It is good practice then to re-record the whole thing on to one unspliced tape to avoid the possibility of a splice coming apart during the performance.

Timing the start of a cue will depend on the speed at which the tape-machine operates. First, the precise position of the play-back head should be ascertained. From this position, measure 3¾in to a point *before* the play-back head. It may be found that this is where the capstan is. If not, mark on the deck the required distance with a coloured dot label.

Run the tape past the play-back head to find the precise position at which the sound effect starts (if the machine has an 'edit' facility this helps enormously, but it can be done by switching the machine to 'play' and slowing the tape past the play-back head). With a chinagraph pencil, mark the back (shiny side) of the tape exactly where the sound starts. Pulling the tape out to a convenient position, affix the cue label to the back of the tape at the mark.

If the label is then set by the coloured dot, it will be similarly 3¾in before the play-back head, and at a running speed of 3¾in per second, exactly one second from the start of the sound. The operator knows therefore that, with the cue label positioned at the coloured dot mark, the sound will occur one second after pressing the starting button. If the running speed is 7½in per second, then the label is set 7½in before the play-back head.

A list of the effects should be made with cue numbers corresponding to effect cue numbers in the prompt book. At the technical rehearsal, volume levels can be set and noted on the list, though there may well be adjustments later when heard during performance to a full house. Depending upon the extent of required effects, the sound operator will either have his own marked prompt book or, if the effects are minimal, a simple annotated list may suffice. In either case, like other departments, he will be cued by the Deputy Stage-Manager. When making an effects tape, it is better to work with normal-play quality tape rather than long-play, which is much thinner and therefore that much more difficult to handle.

Like all else in the theatre, sound effects should be used judiciously. Overdone, or too loud, they become a distraction. If the effect is required to be continuous, like rain or howling wind, unless there are specific reasons (like references to it in the dialogue, for instance) it is better to establish the sound at the beginning of the scene, then take it down to a background level, and bring it up again at the close of the scene.

7 | Costume

The wardrobe department

In mounting a production, the Producer will choose a Director and, probably in consultation with him, engage a Designer, who will have overall responsibility for scenery and costumes and so achieve a harmony of design in the general decor.

That is the ideal. How close the amateur group or society may aspire to this will be governed by its nature and resources. Whether, for example, it is a drama society, which builds its own sets and scenery and has its own Director and Set Designer. The latter may also design the costumes, but more often this will be the province of the Wardrobe Mistress. Perhaps in the majority of cases, financial considerations will make compromise necessary. Actors playing leading characters in modern plays often supply their own wardrobe and between them and the Wardrobe Mistress manage to equip any character parts, maids, butlers, policemen, etc. There will, however, be times when hiring costumes becomes inevitable.

Other societies, and certainly those staging musicals, will hire the whole wardrobe for the production from costume hire firms. What degree of harmony of design is then possible becomes problematical. The scenic contractors usually do not supply the costumes, neither do costume suppliers offer scenery. While both will supply scenery or costumes appropriate to the date and style of the subject, it is a matter of chance whether the scenery and costumes will achieve the perfect blend of harmonious colour.

In some cases, costumes will, to some extent, accord in style and colour, with the original production, as will the scenery also. On the other hand, some scenic suppliers, in constructing sets in one or more sizes, may not have the same colours as the original. Initial enquiries made to both suppliers as to overall colours may be worthwhile but, again, this may be offset by other considerations such as the choice of usual contractors, their nearness and the general business relationship that exists between them and the society.

Often the production will, by its very nature, dictate a harmony. The famous black-and-white scene from *My Fair Lady*, for instance, and shows such as *The Merry Widow*, with its emphasis on evening dress and ballgowns, will not be too far out.

Wardrobe Mistress

Most societies will have a Wardrobe Mistress (or sometimes a Wardrobe Master), who is experienced in sewing, dyeing, and dressmaking, and who has knowledge of materials and accessibility to sewing machines. Add to that a jackdaw's passion for collecting items of clothing from charity shops and jumble sales.

The position of Wardrobe Mistress with a big professional production is no sinecure. She will be skilled in the care and repair of clothes, resourceful, methodical and able to organise and run an important department. She will have her own large room allocated, with hired washing machine, tumble dryer, ironing board and drying racks. She will usually have her own sewing machine. In such a production, the costumes will be hired or especially made and her first concern will be to note and list all items. At initial dress parades or dress rehearsals, while two or three assistants help performers into costumes, pinning here and there for future sewing, the Wardrobe Mistress will be with the Designer or Director out front, to note any alterations or changes decided upon. During the run of the show, she settles into a busy routine of nightly washing, daily ironing and constant repairs.

If the society or group maintains its own wardrobe, she will be with the Director and Set Designer at the initial conference. She will, by fair means or foul, obtain a store-room, with rails, for her collection and will recruit helpers at dress rehearsal and performance times. Her flair for turning odd lengths of material, old skirts, curtains, etc., into cloaks, tunics and medieval tabards, plus the knack of finding the shop with just the right material for those special costumes, will make her an invaluable ally to the whole company.

If the society hires costumes, she will have a list of the players' measurements, and when costumes arrive, enlist some helpers to unpack, distribute and help the players into costumes. She will be able to tell the players how to make minor adjustments themselves and impress on them that they are personally responsible for the safety of the costumes. She will insist on no smoking or carrying drinks about in crowded dressing-rooms. Wardrobe is an important department which plays a major role in the production and the contribution of the Wardrobe Mistress is not to be underrated.

Because of design problems affecting both scenery and costumes, historic and remote period plays do not occur so frequently in amateur drama as do more modern pieces. When they do, the society usually plays safe by hiring. Books of theatre costume design are prolific with drawings, photographs, suggestions and ideas for making Biblical, Greek, Roman, Egyptian, Renaissance and Restoration apparel for both sexes.

No doubt there are many drama societies who can boast a Wardrobe Mistress, with an interest in costume and dress, enthusiastic enough to inspire and oversee the making of historic and period costumes. Certainly this is a fascinating subject in itself and the theatre offers a fine opportunity for its exploitation. With imagination and a little flair, it is amazing what can be achieved with the most unlikely resources. Old bedspreads (candlewick, cotton or satin), lace curtains, sheets, blankets, hessian, long dresses, skirts and dressing gowns can, by the use of dyes and the addition of buckram, wires and trimmings, be transmogrified into costumes that look superb from the front.

Very astutely, Susan Date and Kelvin Watson in their book *Come Down Stage* (Pelham Books, 1971), recommend concentration on basic shape and the silhouette as a starting point for costume making of any period. They also have clever observations on the use of simple shaped pieces of material to emulate a number of garments.

8 | Make-up

A brief guide

Concentrated stage lighting is seldom flattering to the natural face. And certainly for many players, the mere fact of putting on make-up assists greatly in the assuming of a character removed from their usual everyday self.

Make-up is a skilled business that requires study and practical exercise and it is doubtful if many in the amateur world devote much spare time to experimentation. In the professional theatre and on television it has bred its own experts who work wonders with latex and totally transforming prosthetics.

There are excellent books with photographs and diagrams for guidance in this specialised field. For general consideration, it may be sufficient in this context to note that for straight make-up there are a number of alternatives, such as 'Pancake' – a solid cake make-up, in a variety of foundation colours, simply applied with a water-moistened sponge pad. These, with care, may be blended and lips and eyes touched in with liners. There are also tubes of cream-like foundation from Leichner, such as Lit-K, which, when applied, resemble the traditional 'five and nine' make-up. Grease-paint sticks probably remain the most versatile and favoured means. They come in a very wide range of colours and for many, if not the majority of actors, constitute the basis of stage make-up. Because they blend most readily this makes them ideal for character work, especially if changes have to be made during the performance, e.g. growing older, or if more than one part is undertaken.

Basic make-up

A basic straight make-up using grease-paints will usually proceed as follows. The face will first be smoothed over with cream make-up remover, then wiped with a soft cloth or tissues to remove any surplus. This serves both as a protective barrier and assists a more even spread of the colour. An application of No 5 cream colour is then spread thinly and evenly over all the face. This makes a base on which to build the make-up. Next an application of No 9, a brick red, is blended in. This needs to be done sparingly, a little at a time, so just the right shade can be achieved. A light touch of Carmine 1 shaded in on chin, upper cheeks, nose and forehead, just over the nose, may be tried. Applied lightly and with care, this will brighten and give contour to an otherwise flat appearance.

Eyes may have a minimum of light blue (some prefer a lake liner) on the upper lids shading off to the eyebrows. A thin dark line on the upper and lower eyelash lines will define the eyes, but great care must be exercised. Overdone, the eyes will look more like buttons. Eyebrows may be lightly touched in with brown, and lips with carmine. (Men should be very sparing with this and as a rule refrain from outlining the lips. They may prefer No 9 instead of carmine – a smear on the top lip, blended in without reaching the edge, is usually sufficient.) The make-up must be taken up into the hair-line and taken down well below the chin and blended into the natural neck. Hard lines must be avoided, otherwise it will look like a mask.

Finally, a Leichner blending powder of a light shade (which also comes in a range of colours) is applied generously overall with a firm powder-puff to press it gently on to the face. A soft brush is then used to brush off any surplus. Many people prefer a coarse white talcum powder instead of a coloured blending. The purpose of the powder is to absorb the grease, and give a soft matt appearance. Make-up is easily removed after the performance with removing cream and soft towels or tissues.

Character make-up

Successful specialised make-up can be achieved only by study, time and experiment. For reasons of space, this is not the place for a treatise on make-up, but a little guidance may be offered.

Never attempt to make-up in fluorescent light. You need at least one clear 100 watt tungsten lamp, and preferably two: one each side of a good mirror. (A point which does not seem to be mentioned in any books on make-up is that some mirrors are coated on the back with black paint. If possible, avoid these. They give a quite false colour reflection. The ones with a red backing give a much truer reflection.) Study books on make-up. They will all advise the same starting point: examine your face in the mirror. Note where the bone structure manifests itself, e.g. cheek bones, jaw bones and where hollows and lines occur. These are the key points.

Experiment

Obtain the following: some removing cream (Leichner or Crowes Cremine); grease-paint sticks (No 5 Ivory, No 9 Brick-Red, No 7 Chocolate, No 6½ Sallow Grey); liners (No 25 Lake, No 28 Light Brown, No 2 Grey, No 326 Light Blue, No 20 White, and Carmine 1); some cheap white talcum powder preferably coarse, as a too fine powder will produce an unwelcome shine); a good firm powder puff and a soft brush for removing excess powder. Then settle down for a little experimenting.

Age is a matter of redistribution of colour in the following manner. Youth: bright, clear areas with defined eyes, as in 'straight' make-up. Middle age: softer tones. Elderly: rather more No 5 than No 9, emphasise cheek bones with No 20 (white) and tone down lips. Very old: make No 5 dominant, with shadings of lake and light blue in eye sockets. Cheek bones, jaw bones and ridge of nose should be delineated with No 20. These lines should be blended in and never left too defined. Black lines for wrinkles merely makes the face look dirty. Make faces at yourself in the mirror and see where natural creases occur. Then follow the line of the crease with a thin lake liner. This makes the bottom of the crease. On each side now add a thin line of white to emphasise the fold of skin. Blend it in carefully and powder. Lips should be toned down, with two or three tiny vertical lines on the lower lip. However, elderly people are not always a plethora of wrinkles – some are well preserved. It is a matter of observation. Experiment with eyebrows, raising them at the corners or shading them closer together. 'Take out' your natural eyebrows with wet white soap, then cover with No 5 and No 9 and try the eyebrows higher or wider apart.

False hair

Wigs can make a huge difference, but they must be worn with care. If there is a 'skin piece' across the forehead, secure the edge inside with double-sided tape and blend in the skin piece with make-up to match the rest of the forehead. If it is an elderly make-up, the join can be disguised by making it into a wrinkle.

False beards and moustaches, either bought ready made up or constructed with crepe hair, should be attached with spirit gum, before any make-up is applied. Crepe hair is made in a variety of shades. A shade lighter than the natural hair looks more authentic. A blend of colours lends realism, e.g. adding a little of a lighter shade of grey will give a texture. Crepe hair comes in tight plaits. Cut off as much as you think you will need, then stretch it in steam to make it straight. In fact, a better way is to prepare it beforehand by wetting it in hot water and then, using string to tie each end, suspend it with a weight for a few hours. This takes the curl out. When making-up, tease it out into little tufts a little longer than required. Apply spirit gum to the chin, upper lip or sideburns, wherever required. Press the end of the tufts on to the gum. Build up the beard or moustache a little at a time. If it is a beard, don't forget to take it under the chin. When thick enough, press with a damp cloth for a minute. Then trim to the desired shape.

When applying the rest of the make-up, where the edge of the beard meets the face, touch in lightly little dots with a light blue liner to avoid a hard artificial-looking line. With care, instead of spirit gum it is possible to use transparent double-sided tape for crepe hair moustaches and for securing made-up items, beards or wigs. Medium-adhesive quality Lettraset from drawing office suppliers is just right for this purpose.

Leichner have a series of make-up charts which, provided you study the contours of your face and use your judgement, can be very useful. Many professionals keep their make-up sticks in cigar boxes. A piece of thin card, folded accordion-wise with ¾in folds to fit the length of the box, will keep the sticks separate. Another piece of card then placed on top will allow space to keep powder-puffs in.

For those keen enough to observe their fellow citizens, study and experiment, make-up can be an absorbing and worthwhile skill. But it requires time and patience.

In most societies, there is usually a person in charge of make-up and the Director's role is confined to checking that the overall look is satisfactory. However, if there is some outstanding or special effect, he will be involved to a higher degree – perhaps in consultation with the actor and/or the person in charge of make-up.

PART TWO
The Director at Work

9 | *Groundwork*

Information gathering and using

Part One surveyed the qualities it is desirable the Director should bring to his task. It also reviewed the medium and practical environment in which he works. Part Two looks at what he actually does in taking charge and setting up a production.

In amateur theatre, it is rare for a Director to be engaged from outside to direct a play, since most drama groups will have one or more amateur Directors who, in all probability, will be the motivating force behind their existence. For those who would like to direct professionally, the path lies through the theatre schools and academies. There is, however, in this country, a thriving amateur theatre movement and foremost in the field is the National Operatic and Dramatic Association – NODA for short. This association co-ordinates the activities of societies and groups affiliated to it and provides a range of services, such as the hire of librettos, scores and much other information. It also has a list of professional Directors, experienced in the professional theatre, from which societies can choose one to take charge of their production.

There are musical societies and amateur groups who for one reason or another do not choose to avail themselves of the services of a professional and rely on the experienced amateur Director.

Taking charge of a production

What follows is an outline of how a professional Director takes charge and guides the amateur society through to the finished production. The methods and procedures may be of use to the amateur Director seeking to give a professional polish to his work, and to the professional who may contemplate the occasional amateur engagement but who has no prior experience in this particular field.

The kind of production which will be considered will be a typical production by a typical musical or operatic society, exemplified in most cities, towns and communities throughout the country. All that has been described in Part One as applicable to the drama group will be equally relevant to staging the more complicated presentation of the musical play.

The majority of societies will start rehearsals months before production time. These rehearsals will consist of one or two nights a week for learning the solo and chorus musical numbers, under the guidance of the Music Director and possibly a local Choreographer. The Director will come to the society four or five weeks before the production to commence 'floor rehearsals', i.e. the intense nightly rehearsals, to set the scenes, the movements, the chorus numbers and so forth, ready for the performance. To present as complete a picture as possible of the Director's approach it is assumed that he is coming to work with a society for the first time.

Before the end product of the architect's and the builder's process becomes visible to the general gaze, there is a great deal of unseen work. Land surveys, plans and drawings, site drainage, materials and foundations compose the unglamorous groundwork upon which will rise the handsome house, mansion or palace to impress the populace. So too, the successful production, if it is to dazzle the spectator, will be firmly set on unseen, unglamorous groundwork.

For the Director, that groundwork involves hours of sitting at a desk studying the circumstances upon which the structure of the production will be based. It will, roughly, fall into two parts. The first part is concerned with information and processing it as far as possible into visual terms, so that the mechanics become visual. The second part will be the challenging business of matching the mechanics with the more or less unpredictable talent, feelings, beliefs, and responses of individual people.

Gathering the information

The Director's first course of action will be to acquire as wide and detailed a picture as possible of the circumstances likely to affect the production. Perhaps the most effective way of achieving this is by use of the questionnaire. Either by structuring a preliminary visit or subsequently by post, it focusses attention and provides the most reliable method of gathering the information most necessary to the initial planning of a production.

Needless to say, a personal visit, where this can be arranged, will result in a clearer picture of the circumstances under which the Director will be working but, even so, such a visit may be infinitely more worthwhile after the information asked for has been gathered and digested. Obscure points can be cleared up and relevant questions asked. Hopeful assurances can be assessed more readily.

As a general rule, most society decisions are made by various committees and it is as well to tactfully establish with the Secretary that he or she has no objection to direct communication by the Director with the various heads of departments. This can lead to a closer rapport with those concerned and often ensures a more prompt reply to urgent enquiries. Thus names, addresses and telephone numbers of heads of departments are also requested on the questionnaires, three of which are reproduced in the following pages. More space than shown should be allowed for replies on the actual questionnaire, and the comments in square brackets will not appear – they are added here by way of explanation.

1 First Questionnaire: General Information

a Technical

Music Director:
Choreographer:
Society Stage-Manager
Do you have have a Stage Director who 'runs the corner'? Or, in Equity terms, a 'Deputy Stage-Manager', i.e. – not the Prompter or Stage-Manager – who gives all the lighting and stage cues?
[It is surprising the number of societies who do not have a Deputy Stage-Manager to do this essential job. Often stage cues are left to the Stage-Manager and lighting cues to the Electrician, each following cues marked in separate books. This can lead to a great deal of hesitation and sometimes confusion. The correct way is to have all cues given by one person who will have marked his prompt book in consultation with the Director and during the performance will be in communication, preferably by intercom, with the Stage-Manager, Electrician, Fly-men and Follow-Spot Operators who will take their cues from him. In this way one person is then responsible for close synchronisation of all departments. See Chapter Two, Stage Management.]
Property Master or Mistress:
[This is an office often neglected. Its importance should be stressed and attempts made to secure a reliable person in this position. See Chapter 11 Rehearsals.]
Wardrobe Mistress or Master:
Who is supplying scenery?
Address:
Telephone number:
Have they supplied ground plans with dimensions?
Please supply copies
[It can often be arranged for the Director to receive

groundplans from the scenery contractors so that he can check or make enquiries himself.]

b The Company

Apart from named principals,
Number of chorus ladies:
Are they used to movement?
Number of chorus men:
Are they used to movement?

[In some societies the chorus has often only been required to walk on and off, or perform the simplest of arm movements, while the dancing has been done by a separate dance chorus. It is as well to be forewarned if a more animated production is envisaged.]

Is there a separate dance team?
Number of men:
Number of ladies:

c Rehearsal arrangements

[It is of the utmost importance to know in advance just how much rehearsal time you have altogether before drawing up the rehearsal schedule.]

Monday to Friday evenings?
What periods?
Times: 7.15 to 10 p.m.? or?
Sundays?
Afternoon and evening?
Times: 2.30 – 5.30; 6.30 – 9.30? or?
Is there a second room available for split rehearsals?
Is it on the same premises?

2 Second Questionnaire: Staging information

a Venue

Where does production take place?
(Theatre, cinema, hall?)
Is a stage plan available?
Preferably to scale, but at least with dimensions indicated.

If no plan, please supply these dimensions:
proscenium opening:
Depth of acting area:
> If it is possible it will be extremely useful if the sight-lines from the front stalls (or perhaps the widest row of stalls) be included. [See Illustration 10, Sight Lines, on page 85.]

Floats (edge of stage) to setting line:
Or to where there is usually a set of running curtains behind the house-tabs, or the point downstage from where it is usual to set the scenery.
Setting line to last set of lines:
Which side is working side (where curtains are worked)?
P/S (left facing audience):
O/P (right facing audience):
Height to proscenium border:
Off-stage space; in feet, O/P: P/S:
From last set of lines to back wall:
Is there a scene dock?
Is there a prop room?

b Hanging facilities

Is it possible to fly cloths, etc.?
If so, please supply plan of grid, showing number of sets of lines, and indicate where fixed lighting bars and spot bars are:
Height of grid, i.e. stage level up to pulleys from where drapes and scenery are hung.
> [This, compared with proscenium border height, may suggest a method of flying if no regular facilities are available. (See Chapter 13, Flow.]

How many working sets of lines?
Counter-weight or hemp:
Fly gantry or stage level:
i.e. from where scenery ropes are operated
> [If stage level, this may mean one side has to be clear of flats.]

What height of flats usually supplied?

c Staffing

> [Sometimes the production takes place in a professional theatre.]

Is there a professional stage crew?

Is there a professional stage-manager?
Is there a society stage-manager?
What are the usual arrangements for 'get-in' and 'fit-up'?
Sound system available:
Tape deck:
Sound operator:
Any other facilities or useful information most appreciated:

3 Lighting information

Electrician:
Please supply details of installation and facilities:
Plan of existing installation:
What kind of board – how many pre-sets?
How many circuits?
Dimmer?   non-dimmer?
What loading limit on each circuit?
Is there patching facility?
Board [control] on stage or front of house?
If front of house: is intercom available?
Magazine battens – how many, what circuits in each?
Spot bars? – how many, what lantern patterns?
What front-of-house lighting [lantern patterns]?
Follow-spots?
Who operates board: professional? society operator?
Is there a society electrician?
Are colour stocks available?
Are there floats [footlights]?
Is there a ground trough?
What other?
Side floods?
Perches?
Any other information.

Planning the production

The information gathered will be more readily and speedily understood
if it is translated visually. This means (if they are not supplied) making
plans of the stage, sets and lighting facilities. If stage plans are available,
they may not be to the same scale as those supplied by the scenic
contractor (which are frequently mere sketches), in which case it is well

worth the trouble of redrawing both to a mutually compatible scale. One very useful size is ½in:1ft.

The first step is a plan of the stage. This basic stage plan will form a permanent background against which tracing paper can be laid allowing hanging, lighting rig, sets and scenery plots to be quickly traced and all drawn to the same scale. Because of its frequent use (and perhaps to be stored for possible future productions at the same venue) it would be more durable if drawn on architect's linen.

This basic stage plan should show the acting area, off-stage space, sets of lines, existing lighting bars and sight-lines, and any other relevant items (including exit doors and fire hoses, which must not be obscured). It will be clearer if different coloured inks are used to distinguish relevant features.

Assuming this system is adopted, a plan will be developed similar to that shown (Illustration 9). This reproduction in black and white does not convey the clarity of the original, where the lighting bars (together with all electrical indications) are drawn in green, the sight-lines in yellow, and the centre line, the setting line and dimensions in red. Note the zero mark. It is the centre of the setting line. Dimensions to either side, and to backstage and frontstage, are all taken from this centre point. The setting line which indicates the furthest point downstage from which scenery can be set is usually immediately behind the No 1 runners, generally set in a fixed position, though in special circumstances they may be re-positioned. It is never a good idea to dispense with them. Should an emergency arise only the house-tabs will be left, which would give an unwelcome air of finality to an otherwise minor hitch.

It is worth considering the importance of the sight-lines. These are governed by the position of the end seats on the first row of the stalls (or any wider spread of seats) and the position of the proscenium arch. Generally, they will converge so that people sitting in the end seats will have their view of the acting area restricted to an area bounded on their side by a line drawn from their seat, past the proscenium arch to the backdrop. In some theatres the restriction can be considerable, since further back some rows of seats become wider, so that sight-lines taken from those end positions will cut off considerable portions of the acting area. (There is at least one civic theatre where only one third of the whole acting area is completely visible to all the audience.) This is something to bear in mind when grouping for any bit of action important to scene or play (see Illustration 10 on page 85).

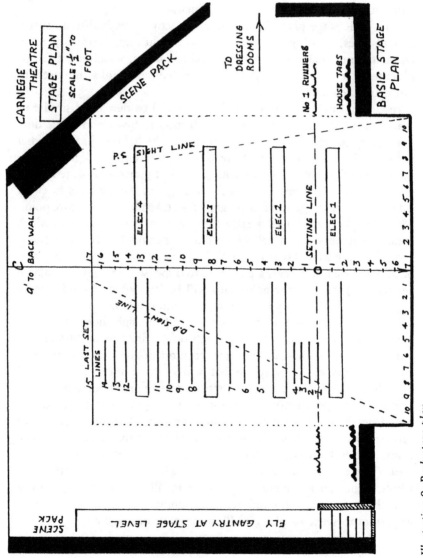

Illustration 9: Back stage plan

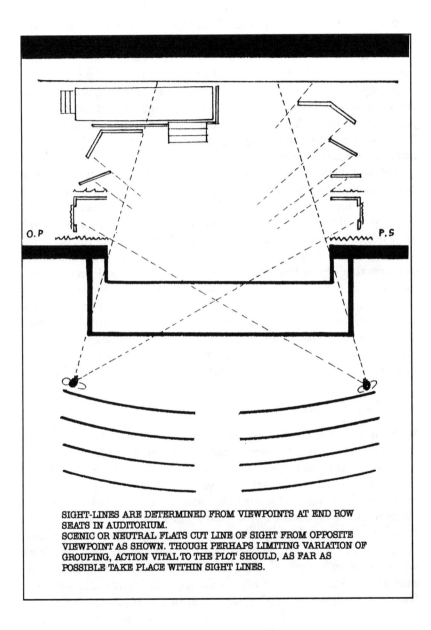

SIGHT-LINES ARE DETERMINED FROM VIEWPOINTS AT END ROW
SEATS IN AUDITORIUM.
SCENIC OR NEUTRAL FLATS CUT LINE OF SIGHT FROM OPPOSITE
VIEWPOINT AS SHOWN. THOUGH PERHAPS LIMITING VARIATION OF
GROUPING, ACTION VITAL TO THE PLOT SHOULD, AS FAR AS
POSSIBLE TAKE PLACE WITHIN SIGHT LINES.

Illustration 10: Sight-lines

Flow

Probably the most important ingredient that a Director can bring to any production, and the one by which he will be judged, is his skill in promoting 'flow'. By this is meant the smooth presentation of the story, free from waits or breaks, so that the narrative flows effortlessly from beginning to end. Flow is most definitely not something added at the dress rehearsal or even the technical run-through. If left till then it is probably too late. Effective flow is built-in during detailed study of all the various elements long before rehearsals commence and involves a great deal of careful planning.

Starting literally from the ground upwards, the first consideration is space. Ingenious visualised groupings and movements will be frustrated if they do not start from a knowledge of the actual space available. Detailed study of the libretto should therefore proceed with full knowledge of the physical requirements and limitations of the proposed sets and scenery. It should be noted that these very limiting conditions can sometimes be rearranged in favour of the visualised presentation, but the time for this is *before* the production reaches the theatre, i.e. here at initial planning not at the dress rehearsal, when it will entail frustrating, wearying and costly delays. To this end, therefore, the next step is to prepare visual aids of the proposed sets. Cardboard models are excellent, and often made for new professional productions, but what is proposed here is less ambitious although equally effective.

Know how it works

With information supplied by the scenic contractors, start by cutting from thin card (to the same scale as the basic stage plan) two-dimensional representations of all the flats, rostra, treads, and so on, which they propose to supply. These are simply to show the *ground area* they will occupy. If the suggested scale of $\frac{1}{2}$in:1ft is used a 3ft x 6ft rostrum will be represented by a $1\frac{1}{2}$in x 3in rectangle of card. Flats are represented by simple strips (say $\frac{1}{4}$in wide) with the corresponding correct width. Then, using these, go through the whole show. With whatever action is required, dialogue, big routine, etc., well in mind, set each scene, deciding where each backdrop will be, the disposition of flats and borders, and noting what masking is required. Preliminary notes on lighting and where spot bars are in relation to the sets should also be made.

This exercise should be repeated several times, always with the object of increasing the speed and flow of the presentation. Where, for instance, scenes may be pre-set, or by the use of trucks, flippers, or a change of backdrop, scene changes may be effected without breaking the flow by having to close the No 1 runners. Changes of backcloths, flats, rostra and masking, off-stage space for scene packs (i.e. flats stored for other scenes) and the possible use of trucks or mobile pieces are all considered and noted. This exercise will reveal where, what size and how many neutral flats, sets of neutral legs, neutral runners or borders will be required for backing, masking and so forth. Often the scenic contractor will assume these items are available at the venue which may, indeed, be true and the society Stage-Manager assumes they will be supplied. Left to chance, adequate masking may be found to be conspicuously missing at the first fit-up. By planning, these requirements are established well in advance.

When the best changes of sets and scenes (i.e. those that contribute most to smoothness and pace) emerge, lay tracing paper over the basic stage plan and trace two copies of each scene, marking the position of backcloths, flats, masking, ground rows, etc., and also the position of lighting bars, spots and so on. (The extra copy will be for the Stage-Manager.)

The hanging plot

At this point, from the sequence of scenes and the disposition of the backdrops, borders and cut-cloths necessary to each scene, the positions of those pieces of scenery required to be lowered in from the 'flies' will emerge. From the basic stage plan a tracing of the acting area showing the positions of the lighting battens and the sets of lines is prepared. On this, all items of scenery to be 'flown' will be indicated against the number of the set of lines on which each is to be hung. This will compose the 'hanging plot' – a vital document which tells the Stage-Manager where each cloth, tabs, border or whatever is to be hung. Carefully prepared, it will save a great deal of time during the 'fit-up' and when scenes are set for the first time.

At this stage it is a useful check for all concerned to draw up a complete list of all cloths, flats, drapes, borders, rostra, treads, and neutral backing pieces required, sending one copy to the Stage-Manager and, most importantly, a copy to the scenic contractors, with a letter confirming the expectation of receiving items as listed. Though no guarantee, this often prevents last minute hassles over missing pieces, or unwanted improvisation.

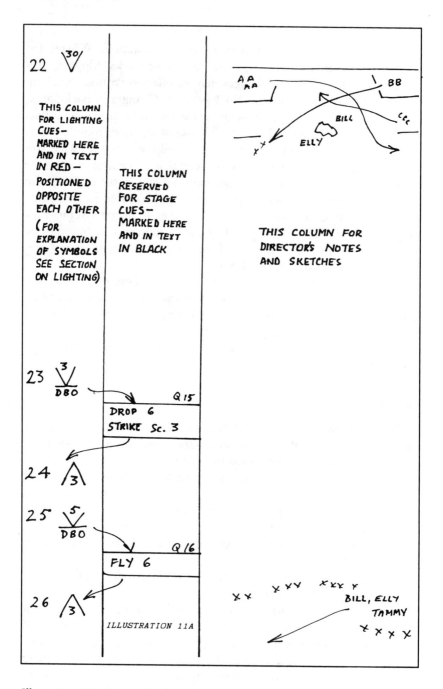

Illustration 11A: Prompt book marked

We keep our memories green
And remember that sweet scene
And our hearts grow ever <u>fonder</u> 22
At the tales so full of wonder.
Yes, Oh! Yes, We'll keep our memories green.

THE MUSIC CONTINUES QUIETLY AS THE COMPANY
PAIR OFF AND SLOWLY DRIFT AWAY INTO THE
GATHERING DUSK. ELLY AND BILL ARE LEFT ALONE.

BILL   There's a fine moon tonight.
ELLY   Uh-uh !
BILL   It looks real pretty over the lake.
ELLY   I've seen it before.
BILL   Not like tonight.
ELLY   What's so special about tonight ?
BILL   It's a Harvest Moon.
ELLY   (She smiles) And what's so special about [...]
    Moon ?
BILL   'Cos a Harvest Moon is a Lovers Moon !
ELLY   You're sure romantic Billy Parsons.
BILL   Sure I am. Wanna see the Moon over the L[...]
ELLY   Well....Oh all right. Jes for a little w[...]

THEY LINK ARMS TO WALK OFF. TAMM[...]
RUSHING ON.

TAMMY   Elly ! Elly !....Per God's sake come qui[...]
ELLY   Tammy ! What is it ? What's the matter ?
TAMMY   It's the House Elly....It's on fire !
ELLY   My God ! Bill, Pa....He'll be trapped !
BILL   <u>Come on !</u> 23   <u>THEY RUSH OFF.</u> 15

> NOTE:
> LIGHTING CUES
> WILL BE MARKED
> IN RED
> STAGE CUES
> IN BLACK.
> TO DISTINGUISH
> THE DIFFERENCE
> IN THIS
> REPRODUCTION
> STAGE CUES
> ARE UNDERLINED
> WITH THICKER
> MARKS

24 SCENE 4 : THE ROAD TO ELLY'S HOUSE.

PATTEN AND GARSTON ENTER

GARSTON   That's sure fixed him. Now mebbe he'll come across !
PATTEN   Yeah ! Yeah ! but get rid of that gasoline can.
    There's folks comin' !

GARSTON THROWS CAN OFF

GARSTON   No one's gonna find that now. We'll just join them
    all, and holler help ! with the rest.

25 <u>THEY ARE SWEPT ALONG BY THE ONCOMING CROWD.</u> 16

26 SCENE 5 : ELLY'S GARDEN.

THE LIGHT OF THE FIRE FLICKERS OVER THE
CROWD GATHERED THERE. ELLY AND BILL ENTER.

Illustration 11B: Prompt book marked

The prompt book

With a reasonable knowledge of the physical mechanics of the production, the layout, areas and entrances of each set, the next requirement is the preparation of the prompt book. By one means or another (perhaps using a second copy), make up an interleaved copy of the libretto, with the text on one side facing a blank page. This blank page is ruled with three columns. On the outside edge a column of about 4cms. Next, a column of similar width, and the rest of the page makes the third (wider) column. What follows may be more readily understood by a glance at the illustrations on pages 88 and 89.

The first column is reserved for lighting cues marked in red. The second column is for stage cues marked in black. The third (wider) column is for brief sketches and notes of the positions and movements of the actors. Sound cues can be added in the lighting or stage columns in green. Lighting cues will be indicated in two places. The word or action in the libretto to be taken as the cue is underlined in red and the number of the cue added. Opposite, in the lighting column, level with the mark in the libretto, will be marked in bold red, the number of the cue, together with an appropriate sign indicating a fade-up or fade-down, with the timing in seconds, or snap-up, blackout, etc. An explanation of symbols is given in Chapter 12, Lighting Design. Similarly, stage cues are indicated in the script in black and in the second column in black. Putting cues as level as possible with cues in the text, avoids confusion. Arrows from one column to another indicate the order in which cues are enacted. It is shorthand for 'Then do this'. (See Illustration 11A on page 88).

In addition to the sound, lighting and stage cues, 'warning cues' will be added later on. These are cues warning the lighting control operator, Stage-Manager, or whoever is involved, that the time for the cue change is approaching and to stand by for action. They must not be too early, since attention may wander; or too late for preparatory action. They are best added in consultation with the Stage-Manager and Electrician during the company rehearsals which they attend specifically to follow the action with their plots, in the last week of floor rehearsals.

The warnings and cues should follow a set pattern. Warning cues should be: 'Stand by lighting cue 15', or 'Stand by stage (or flies) cue 18.' The action cues that follow should stick rigidly to the formula: e.g. 'Lighting cue 15 GO,' or, if it is a stage cue, 'Stage cue 18 GO' or, if simultaneous cues: 'Stage cue 18, Lighting cue 15 GO.' It must be clearly understood in all cases that the operative word is GO.

10 | *Groundwork Continued*

The players are involved

So, in the manner shown, the Director has as much information as possible and has thereby laid the foundation and put up the girders of what he hopes will be a successful structure. But he has not yet finished the groundwork. There is still an even more important element to be incorporated: the actors, musicians and technicians, who will give life and glamour to the whole enterprise. Their participation and co-operation also has to be planned and ordered. This chapter looks at the ways in which this may be most readily and agreeably accomplished.

The Music Director

As has been said, rehearsals of the musical numbers, possibly choreography too, will have been running for perhaps two nights a week for several months under the general guidance of the Music Director, who apart from the mechanical side, is next in the hierarchy. Up until the arrival of the Director, he has been the leader, mentor and generally in charge. To some extent the members of the company will have gained some idea of the nature of the production from his view. It is therefore most important that a good degree of understanding and co-operation between Director and Music Director be established as early as possible.

Following on from his initial study, as outlined earlier, the Director will pinpoint any parts where his advance planning may impinge upon the music. Any ideas involving variation of the printed score should be discussed with the Music Director (by letter or telephone if necessary) as early as possible.

While in opera and ballet the importance of the music is most obvious, regrettably, in some musical productions it has not always been given the same consideration. As has been already stated, 'scene change' music has often been added in the course of the original production for purely mechanical reasons, and can with profit be eliminated in the cause of improved pace in stage setting whenever it proves possible. However, there may be sections of music written to create atmosphere for a scene. Dealing with this can be tricky, since it may have been tailored to the original production with exits, entrances and business arranged for stages much larger than the amateur stage for the current production. This requires careful consideration. For example, it would weaken the effect if music written for the original production to create atmosphere accompanying the entrance of an actor down a grand staircase at the beginning of some solemn scene was eliminated; and it would become ludicrous if attempts were made to speed it up if the grand staircase was, in the present production, but three steps down from a rostrum.

Often scenes open with a great deal of music and business to convey the ambience of a particular location, street, restaurant, or whatever. The production will lose a great deal if the music written to accompany and enhance the action on stage is not matched with movement or, as sometimes happens in less caring direction, even left out altogether.

To match action with what appears to be background music requires care from the Director and co-operation from the Music Director. Sometimes action relevant to the original production will be indicated by words in the score. At times, however, such action may not be apposite for the amateur production; the Director must then invent business appropriate to the present circumstances. If he can read music, his task will be that much easier. Usually scores have bar numbers in which case if, by one means or another, the Director can identify the bar numbers with music as heard, he may be able to create and match the business or action accordingly.

It goes without saying, therefore, that close co-operation between Director and Music Director is highly desirable if not imperative for a successful production. While the Director's view takes precedence, he would be wise to listen carefully to the specialised advice of the Music Director.

The Choreographer

The interpretation of 'choreography' can be somewhat ambiguous. It may refer only to the dance routines of chorus and principals; or it may also include the disposition of the company in ensemble scenes. Sometimes the Director will have reached that position after previous experience as a Choreographer, in which case he will do his own choreography. Perhaps in the majority of cases there is a local dance mistress or master who sets the dances for the society. Even so, the general direction of the routines will be in the province of the Director, so the early co-operation he has established with the Music Director, will be echoed in his early contacts with the Choreographer.

Again, before the actual rehearsals commence, the Director will have as clear a picture of the movement of principals and chorus commensurate with the stage settings as envisaged in the original planning. In this way, he will be able to advise the Choreographer in advance of his ideas concerning the routines of the principals and chorus or dancers, and the setting and stage space available for all the numbers.

It will, perhaps, now become clear why, as mentioned in the section on questionnaires in this chapter, it is important to establish direct contact with the Music Director, Choreographer, Stage-Manager and other heads of departments. Having studied the mechanics and established good levels of communication with those first concerned, other aspects of groundwork planning must be considered so that the actual players, chorus, dancers and performers are all brought into the picture.

Movement and grouping (blocking)

Leaving entrances, movement and grouping to the inspiration of the moment when actually working with the company itself in the short rehearsal periods available with amateur companies can lead to much wasted time, while experimental moves and groupings are tried. And, sometimes, the moves decided upon are not noted down straightaway, thus wasting even more time at subsequent rehearsals if they have by then been forgotten.

Far better to work through the whole thing in advance, making notes and brief sketches. To facilitate this, what is required is some means of visual representation of the entrances and movements of the principals and groups against the proposed sets, without having to scrap and redraw schemes which prove unsatisfactory as the scenes progress. Models are very useful but are time consuming to make, lack portability, and are probably limited to the one production for which they are designed. A simpler facility is required which represents the characters and chorus against the proposed sets, all shown on the stage area. The method described here embraces these features and, in addition to being easily portable, may be used repeatedly for any production.

A plotting board

A sheet of tinplate 18in x 24in is obtained and painted white. This is a convenient size to take a basic stage plan and plans of each setting. It is also a convenient size to sit nicely in the bottom of a suitcase, when necessary. Next, some strips of ferrous oxide (magnetic strips) 5mm wide x 3mm thick, obtained from drawing office suppliers, are cut into 50 small pieces ½in long. Two strips about 18in long serve to hold the plans magnetically on the tinplate 'board'. A smaller piece of tin (in fact a small flat tin box) marked off in sections, 'Principals' and 'Chorus', is used to store the small pieces.

With the basic stage plan on the board, the tracing of the setting being studied is laid on top of it, securing both with the two magnetic strips. The dimensions, sets of lines and lighting bars are easily visible through the tracing. The small squares of oxide representing the characters and chorus, which adhere magnetically to the board, may then be tried out in the most effective positions and are easily repositioned as the scene develops. To differentiate, these pieces are marked with small adhesive coloured spots such as are available in packets in most stationers' shops.

A serviceable scheme might be red for male principals and yellow for female principals, with the name of the character indicated (an initial, or two or three letters). For chorus: blue for men, orange for women, and green for a separate dance team (if there is one). This is an arrangement flexible enough to adapt to most situations. The appropriate questionnaire will have revealed the complement of the company and, having coloured the pieces accordingly, it will be possible to see at a glance the representation on the board where in any full company scene, the principals, the chorus and dancers will be seen to the best advantage. This is particularly important whenever, as in most societies, the women outnumber the men by about three to one. Men, therefore, can be allocated positions in advance to suggest a greater preponderance.

The board can be propped up on the desk in front of the script and the grouping and movements worked out and, when satisfactory, noted down in the third column of the prompt book. The magnetic pieces have the advantage of being able to be moved easily, and are (at the same time) less likely to be accidentally moved, so that the whole thing can be left set up for the next session without the pieces getting mixed up (see Illustration 12 on page 95).

This detailed study, together with a knowledge of the 'mechanics' of the production, means that rehearsals will start and continue on a firm line, with movement strategy, entrances and grouping decided and planned with economy and a minimum of indecision. But this is not all. The shape of the whole production will emerge and assume a firm image in the mind. At the same time, ideas of emphasis and pace will spark off decisions regarding lighting and other matters of presentation, such as ways to eliminate as much as possible the use of the No 1 runners while scenes are changed. Their continual use can be fatal to the desired smooth seamless presentation, summed up in the word flow.

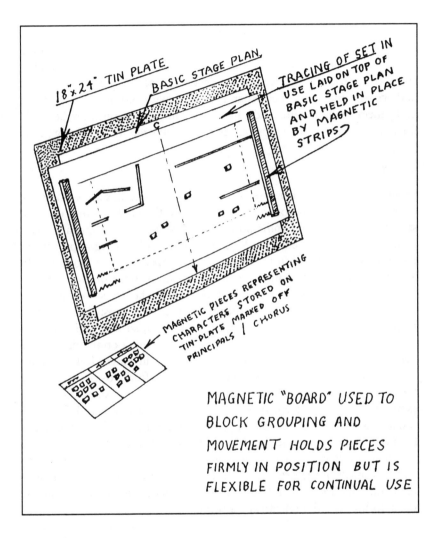

18"×24" TIN PLATE

BASIC STAGE PLAN

TRACING OF SET IN USE LAID ON TOP OF BASIC STAGE PLAN AND HELD IN PLACE BY MAGNETIC STRIPS

MAGNETIC PIECES REPRESENTING CHARACTERS STORED ON TIN-PLATE MARKED OFF PRINCIPALS / CHORUS

MAGNETIC "BOARD" USED TO BLOCK GROUPING AND MOVEMENT HOLDS PIECES FIRMLY IN POSITION BUT IS FLEXIBLE FOR CONTINUAL USE

Illustration 12: Magnetic board for grouping

More about flow will be found in Chapter 13.

If some ensemble scenes involving entrances, exits and movements by the chorus and principals are too big to be sketched in the third column in the prompt book, separate sheets may be used, with the movements marked in inks to match the colours of the various pieces on the blocking board. This can save a great deal of time in the rehearsal room, since entrances, movements and exits are decided in accordance with the sets and scenery and noted beforehand. Parallel with plotting the grouping and general stage pictures, advance notes and suggestions may be made for the guidance of the Choreographer (see Illustration 13 on page 97).

The chorus

From many accounts there are Directors who, in setting scenes where the chorus is involved, announce: 'This is where the crowd comes on. Just sort yourselves out and come on from both sides.' And it appears this is by no means an isolated attitude. This is a most dispiriting approach for those whose contribution to the show is of considerable importance. In any case, a crowd sweeping on from both sides is poor production.

A better way is to make a brief outline of the set showing which entrances may be used for the chorus to enter in groups. At this initial planning stage, names are unlikely to be known, so it is convenient to mark them Group A, Group B and so on. Next, mark on the drawing of the set the position from which each group will enter. Indicate their routes, if and where they will meet and, in their final positions, indicate the size of the group, so that if there are four in Group A show this on the sketch as A A A A; if there are two in Group B show this as B B. This will result in a much more reliable indication of numbers and distribution in the final ensemble picture (see Illustration 14 on page 98).

Having dealt with the technical aspects and made notes on grouping and movement in the prompt book, the next concern is one of the most important and the most difficult. It is the plan of campaign to bring the show to life, i.e. the rehearsal schedule.

The rehearsal schedule

There is rarely enough time in the professional theatre, but in the amateur theatre time becomes the most precious commodity. In the professional theatre, the company can start at ten in the morning and go on late into the night if necessary but, with the amateur company, it must be remembered that those involved probably work during the day

```
┌─────────────────────────────────────────────────────────────┐
│                                                             │
│  HUDDERSFIELD A.O.S.        Production : MY FAIR LADY        │
│  A.B.C. November              DIRECTOR: GEOFF MORRIS         │
│  ─────────────────────────────────────────────────────────  │
│                                                             │
│  NOTES FOR CHOREOGRAPHER. To amplify notes already          │
│  in script, and indicate the style of the scene.            │
│  ─────────────────────────────────────────────────────────  │
│                                                             │
│  1  ACT I Sc.1 : Libretto P.14. Score P. 6 - 7              │
│     Buskers : 2 Men and Girl : Simultaneous                 │
│     routine for three (to get them on stage and             │
│     collect 'pitch') - repeat 8 bars if required.           │
│     8 bars soft shoe together, then 8 bars for              │
│     Girl solo, while boys remove jackets,                   │
│     mufflers and bowler hats leaving them in                │
│     trousers and singlets (like strong men). Then           │
│     all three attempt simple balancing trick -              │
│     girl on shoulders - which fails, one boy                │
│     falling into Freddie, which will take us into           │
│     the action.                                             │
│     Leave the fall until I arrive, since this               │
│     will involve business for crowd reaction.               │
│  ─────────────────────────────────────────────────────────  │
│                                                             │
│  2    ACT 1 Sc. 1 : Libretto P. 23 Score P. 14 - 21         │
│                                                             │
│       RECITATIVE. Eliza comes centre. Cockneys from         │
│       P/S to work lines to her, then cross to O/P           │
│                                                             │
│       1st Coro : Eliza solo, while Cockneys set up          │
│       'dining table' with dust cart (such a street          │
│       sweepers use). Dustbins as chairs, Newspapers         │
│       as Napkins, et cetera.                                │
│                                                             │
│       2nd Coro : Mime business of dining 'posh.'            │
│       Eliza join them, miming 'hostess' sampling            │
│       wine, et cetera.                                      │
│                                                             │
│       3rd Coro : Soft shoe with street sweepers (as         │
│       though they are cabaret). Eliza joins them.           │
│       Cockneys at table pack up props and turn cart         │
│       into a cab.                                           │
│                                                             │
│       Finish : Eliza mounts cab and is taken off in         │
│       procession.                                           │
│                                                             │
└─────────────────────────────────────────────────────────────┘
```

Illustration 13: Examples of notes for choreographer

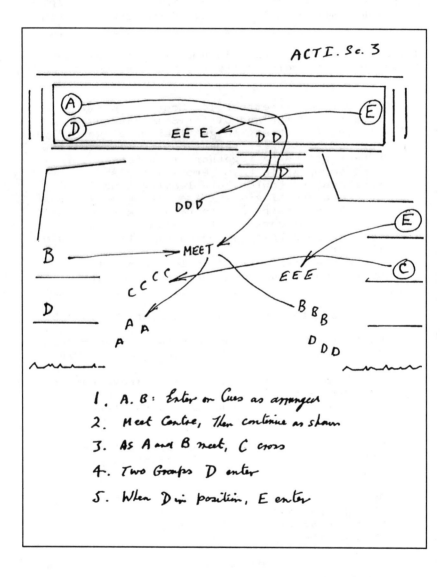

ACT I. Sc. 3

EE E   D D

D

D D D

B ———→ MEET

C C C C

D

A A
A

E

C

E E E

B B B

D D D

1. A. B: Enter on Cues as arranged

2. Meet Centre, Then continue as shown

3. As A and B meet, C cross

4. Two Groups D enter

5. When D in position, E enter

Illustration 14: Chorus entrance plots

and give of their free time in the evenings. This may mean two and a half hours each night during the week with, it is to be hoped, the added luxury of Sunday afternoons and evenings. Over four weeks, this amounts to eight full days compared to a professional period of six or eight weeks. It is thus absolutely necessary to make the best use of every minute of the all too short evening sessions – usually 7.30 to 10 p.m. It will take an appreciable time to devise the rehearsal schedule. Allow two or three days at least.

Here are some useful principles to keep in mind:

1   It must be comprehensive, leaving nothing to the final dress rehearsal.

2   It must maintain the company's interest (as the performers are not paid).

3   While those sufficiently keen are welcome at all times, it should call people only when they are required – many people may have business or family commitments which demand their attention.

4   It must be economical with precious rehearsal time (another reason for careful advance planning). There is often a problem with timekeeping and making a prompt start to rehearsals. Whatever time is scheduled for the rehearsal to start, that time is usually interpreted as the time of arrival. It may help to allow for ten or fifteen minutes being wasted at the beginning. A plea for promptness, on the schedule and in person on the first night, may help but generally, for all the reasons in the world, it is a red letter day when rehearsals actually start at the time scheduled.

Constructing the schedule

With the preceding in mind, the first thing to do is to list those items which are going to require the most time to set: full ensemble numbers, big routines, and the like. It will help full attendance if these can be allocated to the evenings which prior to the Director's arrival have been chorus rehearsal nights. Dialogue or business sessions, solo numbers and particular scenes should also be listed. Double check to ensure that every bit of the action has its allotted time; what appears to be the simplest phase can often throw up unexpected problems. Then estimate the time each item is likely to require to set.

The next thing is to set out all the items into various evenings separating, if and where possible, dialogue sessions from those involving the chorus or even the Music Director, so that as far as possible no one is called if he or she is not involved. Additionally, divide the evening into sessions so that people are not sitting around waiting. Generally, this concern for people's time is appreciated and can result in prompt attendance at the times for which they are called. Sometimes there will be the bonus of a separate room which can be enormously helpful, allowing dialogue and solo or chorus numbers (with the help of the Choreographer or Music Director) to be rehearsed on the same evening. As well as allocating time for setting numbers, dialogue and the like, it is necessary to allow time for progressive revision, otherwise routines will be forgotten as people try to absorb new numbers.

The very recognition of all the factors involved in organising the rehearsal time available most economically, and in keeping all informed, will suggest, if not dictate, the shape of the rehearsal schedule. It may have five columns. The first will show the date and time. The second will be entitled 'Specific', i.e. what is to be rehearsed. The third column will be 'Characters', i.e. those required to attend. The fourth will be 'Chorus/Dancers'. And the last will be 'Technical', detailing what technical people will be required, e.g. Music Director, Choreographer, Pianist, Prompter or Property Master (see Illustration 15 on page 101).

If the total period of rehearsal is the usual four weeks, aim to have everything, however roughly, set by the end of the second week. The third week can then be used for revising, polishing, and running various sections in sequence. The fourth week can be most advantageously spent in revising whatever needs attention. If on schedule, the fourth week may run as follows:

Monday: Act One in sequence, as far as possible without stopping. Technical people to attend. (See Chapter 11. Rehearsals).
Tuesday: Act One revised as noted from Monday.
Wednesday: Act Two (and Act Three if it exists) in sequence, without stopping. Technical people to attend.
Thursday: Revise Acts Two (and Three) as noted from Wednesday.
Friday: First dress rehearsal (i.e. costumes only).
Saturday: Get-in and fit-up in theatre (if possible).
Sunday: Morning: Orchestra Rehearsal. Complete fit-up and focus lanterns.

Afternoon: **Rehearsal rooms**: company revise with Music Director and Choreographer.

Theatre: lighting and setting rehearsal, with Director, Deputy Stage-Manager, Stage-

W.A.D.A.M.S. Spring Production . Carnegie Theatre . Workington

"HELLO DOLLY" : Director : GEOFF MORRIS · REHEARSAL SCHEDULE

Rehearsal Period : 7.30 to IO P.M. This schedule is designed to make the best possible use of available time. Please make every effort to attend as called. Any absence results in the loss not only of the original session, but a second. Would you please arrive at a few minutes before 7.30 so that we can actually start on time.

PRINCIPALS : Please bring pencils for marking at early sessions.

This presentation requires close co-operation between artistes and Stage Management. Technical People are requested to attend at the First Rehearsal, as indicated, to check and discuss staging arrangements.

DATE	SPECIFIC	CHARACTERS	CHORUS DANCRS	TECHNICAL
FEB Mon I9	7.30 : Run thro' all Nos. as rehearsed to date	All Principals	Chorus	Music Director Pianist Choreographer
	8.45 : To check and Discuss Staging etc.	All Technical People : Stage Manager, Stage Director, Wardrobe Mistress, Property Master, Electrician, Business Manager.		
Tue 20	7.30 : Act I Sc. I	Dolly, Ambrose		M/D, Pianist
	7.45 : Sc. 4 Feedstre	Dolly, Vand, Cornelis Barney, Ermgd, Ambrse		
Wed 2I	7.30 : Ribbons	Mrs. Molloy		M/D, Pianist
	7.45 : Hat Shop & Motherhood	Minnie, Molloy, Corn, Barney, Dolly, Vand		M/D, Pianist
Thu 22	7.30 : Sunday Clothes		Chorus	M/D, Pianist Choreographer
	7.30 : Room 2			

Illustration 15: Example of rehearsal schedule

Manager, stage and lighting crews.
Evening: **Full Dress Rehearsal** with full technical complement.

A fuller explanation of this will be found in Chapter 11, Rehearsals.

A copy of the proposed schedule is then sent to the society Secretary
for verification, after which copies are distributed to every member of
the society including the technical people, so that all concerned have a
minimum of two or three weeks' notice of when they will be required.
The rehearsal schedule is the plan of campaign for the whole effort of
getting the production working. It is the end product of very careful
planning and preparation. On it depends a very great deal. It should
keep all concerned aware of what is happening: when they are required
and what for, and when props are required and what for. Carefully
drawn up, it will ensure smooth rehearsals and hassle-free final
rehearsals. If strictly adhered to, it will go a very long way to ensure the
success of the final production. It is also the Director's best friend when
rehearsals actually commence.

11 | *Rehearsals*

Organising for success

For those imaginative people who have a love of theatre and have experienced its spell, creative rehearsals (and all rehearsals should in some degree be creative) can often be almost as exciting and satisfying as the actual performance.

When the right atmosphere has been created players, carried along by the tension of the moment, will unconsciously achieve the dramatic characterisation aimed for. At such moments the magic of acting, the enchantment of theatre, become manifest and there is an air of excitement, a sparkle in the eye and a realisation that that wondrous thing, an 'act of theatre' has taken place. And what a tremendous effect this can have on the enthusiasm of all concerned. Such experiences of the craft of theatre are infrequent enough in well-run rehearsals. In sloppy, haphazard rehearsals it is unlikely that they will ever occur – even later during performance!

Directors of avant garde groups with skilled actors and long-running rambling rehearsals can enjoy the luxury of commencing with hazy ideas and experiment with suggestions and notions from the cast. No such luxury attends the Director who has to mount a full-scale musical in four weeks of part-time efforts by amateurs, however dedicated and keen they may be.

If rehearsals start with the Director having a pretty clear concept of the whole show, people are usually ready to trust his judgement and guidance providing they feel that it is based on a sound knowledge of the situation in hand. The aim of the preparation described here is designed to justify that trust. This does not mean that there is no room for creativity on the part of the players. In putting themselves forward for parts at auditions, they usually go for those characters which they believe they can portray and will sometimes bring valuable ideas to strengthen the characterisation. Often however, the characterisation has to be suggested, nurtured and brought out. Not infrequently the Director encounters genuine talent and, when that happens, he will recognise it immediately and accord it the respect it deserves.

The first rehearsal

The first rehearsal is most important. Director and company will weigh one another up, and first impressions are vital. If the Director can appear approachable, friendly and knowledgeable about the business in hand, it will go a long way to securing the trust of the company upon whose co-operation he must ultimately rely. The preliminary preparations outlined may already have gone some way to create confidence in his capabilities.

If the rehearsal scheme suggested here is followed it will generally proceed along these lines. As the rehearsal schedule illustrated indicates, the first rehearsal is divided into two sessions. The main idea is to get to know the players, the chorus, the officials and the technical people, and to create the atmosphere of a team effort. In the first session it is a good idea to simply sit back, make notes and allow the Music Director to take the company through all the numbers so far rehearsed, including principals' solos and any dance routines on which the Choreographer may have worked. After that, a brief talk about the rehearsal schedule, explaining anything that needs clarification or emphasising (like the importance of attending when called) pointing out the extreme pressure of time and drawing attention to the fact that efforts have been made not to call anyone who is not actually required. It is useful to make the point that absence when called not only wastes time at that session, but also at a second, when time has to be spent going over again what should have been completed at the first session.

Team-work

To emphasise that the success of the show depends upon team-work, it is a good idea to invite those who wish to remain, but to point out that the remainder of the session will deal with aspects of concern to the technical people, whose contribution is of considerable importance. The rest of the evening is then spent with the Music Director, Choreographer, Wardrobe Mistress, Stage-Manager, Stage Director (or Deputy Stage-Manager), Electrician, Property Master and Business Manager.

With the plans of the stage to hand, go through all the sets, laying the tracings of the various sets on the stage plan, discussing each and the changes and scenery involved. Discuss the hanging plot and other relevant details, such as when the scenery will be delivered, and when it will be hung and fitted up, pinpointing as far as possible precise dates and times.

With the Electrician, discuss dates and times for rigging, focussing and colouring up. Most importantly, what is required from him is the precise number of circuits to be used and how they will be arranged and distributed on stage and front of house. Usually a meeting can be arranged with him on site. Discuss any problems with the Wardrobe

Mistress, and check with the Property Master the arrangements for properties and also what will be available (actual or substitutes) for rehearsal sessions as indicated in the schedule. The Music Director, Choreographer and Business Manager will doubtless all weigh in with comments and problems.

It is useful to point out that, as indicated in the schedule, on two evenings during the final rehearsals in the rehearsal room, when going through Acts One and Two in sequence, all technical people will be required to attend.

The Director should take care that all future rehearsals take place in areas (marked out by tapes, chairs or whatever) that correspond to the layout of the proposed set. Entrances should be in correct positions and the width and depth of the acting area should correspond to the stage plan. A retractable steel tape-measure is a valuable accessory here.

It is as well to remember that for the company the rehearsal is in the nature of a social occasion. It is their leisure time. They will be friends and will have enjoyed past social occasions together. There will, therefore, be a natural tendency to chat, reminisce and laugh. There will be a pleasant atmosphere conducive to good relationships, relaxed, and (one might suppose) ideal for the business in hand. And to a large extent it is, but the Director will be under pressure, always working against the clock – there never is enough time – so conducting rehearsals over a four week period requires a tactful firm hand and discipline.

Split rehearsals

The chorus may maintain an active interest as long as they have a routine to learn and practise, but when they have to sit back for the principals' dialogue, there is a tendency for talk and chatter to build up and they have constantly to be reminded that what is being rehearsed is equally important. This is a cogent reason for split rehearsals.

A second room, however small, can be invaluable in this respect. The Music Director and Choreographer can rehearse the chorus numbers which have been set, while the principals can perfect the dialogue and business in comparative quiet. It is here too that the Director can most effectively convey the concept – the style of the show in the matter of movement, business and pace. There is opportunity to get to know the temperament of the principals, and how best to adjust that to the characterisation required. They are all individuals and their understanding of the situation, the demands of the part, will result in a kind of compromise between what the Director has in mind, and what they are able to come up with. A little knowledge of the psychology of individual differences is useful here, but at the very least it should be remembered that people have different temperaments and require different approaches, especially in the exposed situation which the actor (professional and amateur) is constantly coping with.

Often people will say and do things as indicated in the script without realising why they are doing or saying them, and it is heartening to see (after a little exploratory chat) understanding dawning and the difference this makes to their portrayal, and to the scene as a whole. Occasionally a situation arises where a player has a particular view of a character, perhaps from a previous production under other circumstances. Once again this will be a matter of give and take within the overall view.

In the initial stages, players will, even if they think they know their lines, generally carry their scripts. This is useful, since they can mark in pencil moves or entrances which arise. Usually, however, characterisation and pace can start to develop only when scripts are no longer carried. Many people find that the moves and physical action help in memorising lines, so the sooner active rehearsals start, the better. In memorising lines, before floor rehearsals, a tape-recorder can be of assistance. So too can the reading of lines last thing at night before going to sleep. A most potent way of concentrating upon and absorbing lines is to write them out in longhand.

Pace and timing

One of the most difficult things to convey is the art of timing. It is this that, in so many instances marks the difference between the professional and the amateur. After one has done what one can in the basic matters of diction, projection and attack, the essential thing in any speech is *what is going on in the mind* – the emotions and thoughts that give rise to the words.

This, more than anything else, leads to an understanding of the art of timing. Identify the emotion, the feeling that prompts the words and you are more likely to get the pace right. There is more to it of course: there are also the basic requirements of projecting the voice, of pausing and of judging audience reaction. This is an art that marks the so-called 'natural' actor. It is also something that is learned and perfected by experience.

Complementary to timing is the appreciation of pace. It is in this aspect that the Director can play a vital role. The individual, intent on putting all he can into his or her personal contribution, will not always appreciate the overall effect at which the Director aims. Neither is the concept of pace always understood. Too often it is thought to imply speaking more quickly, which can lead to gabbling, when in fact it has all to do with maintaining interest, where a pause can be as important as the quick pick-up of cues. Perhaps nowhere is this so important as in comedy, particularly in the skilled business of visual comedy, where in the hands of great clowns, the pause can convey a whole range of emotions, without a word spoken.

In later stages of rehearsal it is useful to time with a stop-watch the various sections of the show, the ensemble numbers and especially the dialogue and business. This can assist in arranging staging, costume changes and lighting cues and, importantly, in keeping the show running to time. It is useful too if it becomes necessary to make cuts at some future performance time.

Ensemble

It has already been described how entrances and grouping of the chorus have been worked out. In the actual rehearsal, slight alterations in the groups to get the best disposition of heights and so forth can be made and scenes set with a minimum of time. It is also important, if a song is involved, to check the disposition of the chorus in the groups with the Music Director, since it may well be necessary to keep the various voices (tenors, contraltos, basses, and so forth) together – compromise may be necessary.

Chorus reaction

If a social gathering is to be represented, it is likely that, if not carefully set, there will be immobility on the part of the ensemble or the absurdity of a lot of people apparently talking at the same time with no-one listening. If left to the imagination of those concerned it is also likely that everyone's mind will have suddenly gone blank.

As a stimulus for couples and groups, therefore, a suggestion by Rodney Bennett (the writer on amateur theatre) made some years ago, is still effective. A simulated conversation may be set that goes like this:

A: 'I say, did you know that in the alphabet B follows A?'

B: 'Really? Then it's probable that the next letter will be C.'

A: 'That's right. And, as you may have heard, the next letter is D.'

B: 'I see. So that E will naturally follow . . . .'

Another ploy is the two times table:

A: 'D'you know, I've just heard that two times two is four.'

B: 'Good Heavens; does that mean that two threes are six?'
A: 'Yes indeed. And it goes further – it turns out that two fours amount to eight . . . .'

If the actors are asked to simulate varying degrees of surprise, or interest in this way, the effect can be quite convincing.

Often the script calls for more positive chorus reaction, mirthful or angry. Once again it is fatal to leave it to the spur of the moment. Inevitably nothing will come, or if it does, it will be tardy and a thoroughly unconvincing 'Ruh... ruh..'. The following procedure, developed by the author, has been successful.

Allow a few moments for each member of the ensemble to think of a sentence of about six or seven words on a subject of their own choice. The Director should ask them to try to include lots of hard consonants where possible – this will give edge to the sentence. Then to make sure they have produced a sentence, each member should say the sentence aloud. The sentences need not be related to the scene. The combined voices will obscure the actual words, and what comes over will be the emotion.

On cue, everyone should repeat simultaneously the sentences half-a dozen times. Then, the exercise should be repeated in various emotional ways: anxious whispering, with laughter inflexions, angrily, then shouted; and, finally, with clenched fists, arms waving like an angry mob. A little time spent drilling this exercise, jumping from one way of projecting to another, gives the chorus members the confidence and readiness to respond without waiting for one another to start, and overcomes that blankness of mind when reaction to the plot is called for.

Do *not* 'act natural'!

It is important to impress upon chorus members that their presence in any scene is *not* incidental. Too often they have been given the impression that they are there 'to make up the crowd' or 'to make up a background' and not all that essential to what is happening with principals downstage. They should never at any time be told to come on stage and 'just act natural'. Such advice is completely at variance with the highly unnatural situation in which anyone on stage finds himself.

Instead, the advice should be to be conscious at all times of what the show is all about, the ambience of the particular scene in which they are appearing, and their relationship to the action of the principals. In other words, just as much as the principals, they are *required to act*. There is a technique which they should learn and practise. It involves an artistic discipline – a concentration on the demands of the immediate situation. This means that they will switch from, say, background simulated conversation, to paying attention to the principals' dialogue, and the appropriate response which this calls for, be it anger, laughter, or a song. It is well worth pointing out that those who look so natural and relaxed on stage achieve this appearance only by absorbing into their subconscious, through constant rehearsal and practice, the discipline of stage-technique.

If the members of the chorus are convinced in this manner of their integral importance to the scene, it will make an enormous difference to their enjoyment of their role and result in enhancement of ensemble scenes. There is one other thing to be watched. If there is a situation of tense concentration, be it a moment of dramatic dialogue or a passage in a song, where attention is focussed on a soloist, any thoughtless or 'unconscious' movement in the back row, where someone raises a hand to scratch his nose or smooth her hair or whatever, can jerk attention away from a principal in a moment of stillness in song or dialogue, and breaking the tension can effectively diminish the whole scene. That is why the chorus must be induced at all times to remember technique, *that is to act and never to 'act natural'*. And this must be insisted upon during rehearsals. If not, the technique will not be learned.

Rehearsals should develop. As mentioned earlier, the aim is to get everything, solos, ensemble numbers, dialogue, etc., set by the end of the second week. During the third week, as well as revising, sections of the show should be rehearsed, so people get to know what follows what.

A word about the Prompter. In a musical where the interpolation of musical numbers results in passages of dialogue being much shorter, the presence of the Prompter at every rehearsal is not so vital as it would be in the case of a straight play. Nevertheless, at all dialogue rehearsals the Prompter should be present both for his or her benefit and that of the actors. The actor's performance can be ruined if he is irritated by a Prompter who continually mistakes pauses for business or dramatic effect for memory lapses. The Prompter needs to know the play and the style of the players, knowledge which is only gained at dialogue sessions. While the job is often regarded as unrewarding, it requires a patient and appreciative intelligence. Certainly by the third week, when continuity is important, the value of a good Prompter becomes evident.

The Property Master will also be involved. Where props are concerned, they or adequate substitutes should be available. The players should be able to handle the props they will be using during the performance. Much time can be wasted at dress rehearsals if they have to get used to the props for the first time.

Useful practice

In the later stages of rehearsal, if rehearsal rooms are large enough to permit, there is a practice which is invaluable. The space should be wide enough to allow the sets to be marked out across the room's narrow width. With the piano, Music Director and Director placed in the middle of the room, they face the first set marked out with tapes, chairs or whatever, at one end of the room, with the next scene behind them at the opposite end of the room. At the end of one scene, they quickly turn and face the other way and the company carry on with the next scene at the opposite end without having to break for the set to be cleared and the next set up. While this scene is played, some of the members will clear the first set and arrange the third and so on, so that the Act can proceed without stopping. This allows the players to get to know the time between their entrance in the various scenes and all concerned to gain a better knowledge of the continuity and flow.

Dos and Don'ts

DON'T: Force a player who is having difficulty with any particular bit of dialogue or business. A little break and coming back to it when no one else is there can work wonders.

DON'T: Under any circumstances make a player feel ridiculous by exaggerating something he is doing wrong. No one likes to be made to look foolish in front of his friends and peers.

DON'T: When a rehearsal is flowing be too pedantic about every precise word: let it flow and mention it later.

DON'T: Let the chorus or principals make entrances from the edge of the set in rehearsal. They should start from a few feet away. This enables them to appear to walk on naturally and not 'pop' on like rabbits. It will also be more like conditions on the actual stage and will result in more accurate timing.

DON'T: Allow a player to lower his voice. It is all right for experienced professionals to 'save the voice' but let one amateur lower his voice, or forget to project and it will spread like a disease. Soon everyone will be muttering and the pace and attack will go.

DON'T: Allow the chorus to 'slide' into the first words of a number – attack it! – although, of course, the Music Director or

Chorus Master will most likely have seen to this.

DON'T: Allow a would-be comic to ruin a dress rehearsal by clowning about to exaggerate an ill-fitting costume. Deal with it immediately.

DO: If two principals have a tender scene involving embracing and kissing, do make a positively stern announcement beforehand that it is not easy to rehearse a love scene before a lot of people, that you expect that everyone will co-operate by being quiet and not to spoil the atmosphere with any kind of comments or noises.

DO: Rehearse any particularly tricky bits of dialogue or business with the principals concerned first without the rest of the company present. It will give them confidence.

DO: Emphasise (and it will have to be repeated) that when the chorus leave the stage, the first ones *keep going* – and so allow the others space to get off. All too often the first ones off will, as soon as they leave the stage, stop and find much to talk and laugh about, leaving those still on the stage to push their way through.

DO: When the chorus have to exit angrily or laughing encourage them to *keep it going* until they are well off stage and not to stop as soon as they are out of sight.

DO: Encourage whenever possible. It creates confidence.

As mentioned in the section referring to the rehearsal schedule, in Chapter 10, Groundwork Continued, it may be of value to consider more fully here the fourth week of rehearsal. In many societies the Stage-Manager, Electrician and others do not attend rehearsals. In fact, often the first they see of what actually happens in the show is at the dress rehearsal. It is not at all uncommon for the lighting to be left until then too. If costumes, props, follow-spot operators and Prompter also make first appearances at this event it is not to be wondered at if some dress rehearsals run on chaotically far into the night. They need not and should not.

Technical people should be brought into the proceedings well in advance of the final rehearsals. It is part of the Director's responsibility to see that they are integrated into the rehearsals. By the end of the third week, the Director should have prepared the board lighting plot and the follow-spot operators' plots. The Stage-Manager will already have his plans, and the Deputy Stage-Manager will have a duplicate of the prompt book with the stage and lighting cues marked. The Prompter and Property Master should also be present.

On the Monday of the fourth week, Act One is taken through as far as possible without stopping (the presence of the Prompter will be valuable to this end). The Deputy Stage-Manager ideally seated next to the Electrician, can check the cues, and the Electrician, with stop-watch, can time his changes. The Deputy Stage-Manager will also, at this stage, be able to mark in his prompt book the stand-by warning cues – checking with the Stage-Manager if necessary. The follow-spot operators (for whose benefit the characters will have been previously identified) will follow the action with their plots. At the end of the session any technical points raised can be discussed and dealt with.

On Tuesday Act One is revised with the company only. On Wednesday, Act Two is revised with the technical people present as before. On Thursday Act Two is revised with the company only. The technical people will now have a good idea of what the show is all about and be familiar with and able to follow their plots. They will have some understanding of the scenery and lighting changes when they come to convert this into physical action.

First dress rehearsal

Friday, even if it is still in the rehearsal room, will be the first dress rehearsal. The company will have been advised that this is likely to be a long affair while they try on costumes and give the Wardrobe Mistress and her assistants the opportunity of making notes for alterations, etc. Most importantly it is going to save a great deal of time at the final dress rehearsal. The novelty of the costumes will have gone, alterations will have been made and more serious attention to the business of the performance itself will be possible.

If arrangements can be made for scenery to be got in the venue on Saturday, the Sunday rehearsal schedule will probably run as follows:

Morning: Fit-up and rig lighting.
               Orchestra rehearsal.

Afternoon: **Rehearsal room**: Company with Music Director and Choreographer for revision.
               Theatre: Lighting and setting rehearsal with Director, stage and lighting crews.

Evening: **Theatre**: Final dress rehearsal, make-up *as performance.*
               Full technical complement and orchestra.
               Interval time as performance.
               As far as possible *no stopping.* Notes at conclusion.
               Starting time as agreed (this may be later than performance

time depending upon how the fit-up and lighting has progressed).

When circumstances permit, every effort should be made to conduct this rehearsal as if it were a public performance. Let the running of the rehearsal be in the hands of those who will be doing it on the night of the first performance.

However, while every effort should be made to run the dress rehearsal as much like a public performance as possible, if there have been technical troubles during the fit-up, and time is short, then it may be as well to arrange with the company that if there are hold-ups during a scene, when that scene finishes they should remain on stage, i.e. they should not proceed with costume changes, nor should the stage staff change the set until the trouble has been dealt with. Then, when stage and lighting cues are ready, play the last minute or so of the scene again and go forward with the changes into the next. This will ensure that scenery and costume changes will take place in the times allowed for in the performance. The Director should also, at times when there are no lighting or stage cues to be checked, take a quick walk around front of house to check the sight-lines and general appearance of the stage from the stalls and circle.

During the whole period of rehearsals the Director will have to make decisions. As far as possible he must be decisive. This will be possible if he has done his desk-work adequately and carries a clear picture of the finished show in his mind. Indecision can be fatal. It will breed uncertainty, distrust and perhaps sew discord.

But there also comes a stage when, however much he may want to alter, adjust or otherwise interfere, the wise Director will resist the urge and allow the show to settle down and the players to adjust to one another and to the music. This stage should be reached before the show goes into the theatre. The players will have quite enough to cope with in adjusting to the actual sets, the stage, the lights, the change of acoustics and the whole somewhat frightening ambience of the theatre, without trying to remember changes which the Director may then and there decide. Of course there may have to be some adjustments dictated by unforeseen circumstances. It is part of the Director's job to minimise these as much as possible.

In the theatre

Many contracts call for the Director to rehearse the company for four weeks and then to remain for a full week to keep an eye on the actual performances. This last requirement is an agreeable arrangement for the Director, allowing him a lot of free time to enjoy the local views during the day and to swan about in the theatre at night looking important, or even (Heaven forgive him!) to make fiddling adjustments to the performance.

It is, however, a far more valuable arrangement, where circumstances of the venue allow it, for the fifth week to be given over to rehearsals in the theatre and the Director to leave after seeing the first public performance. If he has done his work adequately and has conducted one good technical and two dress rehearsals on stage with the final one run as a performance, he should be able to leave the show in the knowledge that it will run smoothly without any further interference from himself. This is of far greater value to the actual performance (and the society's perception of detailed stagecraft) than the Director's ineffectual presence at the back of the stalls or in the bar during the performance week.

The ideal situation

It may be useful to describe how this valuable fifth week can be used. Rehearsals for the fourth week will follow the pattern as already described, except that on the Friday, instead of an all-too-soon first dress rehearsal, attention can be given to any sequence that needs extra care. On the Saturday, it is often possible to get the scenery into the theatre and to get much of the hanging done. On the Sunday morning the Stage-Manager and crew can complete the fit-up while the Electrician and his helpers colour-up and rig the lanterns as indicated on their plots. It is often possible for the Music Director to arrange a full orchestra rehearsal in the theatre too.

During Sunday afternoon and evening, while the company either revises as necessary, or goes through the entire show in the rehearsal room, the Electrician can focus the lanterns.

So the fifth week's rehearsals will run like this:

MONDAY: **Rehearsal room:** Final rehearsals and revise as required.

Theatre: Complete fit-up, mark stage, etc. Complete focussing lanterns, (stage and lighting crews).

TUESDAY: **Theatre** (dressing rooms): Company wardrobe call (Wardrobe Mistress and assistants). This gives ample time for adjustment of costumes and any replacements from the costumiers. Artistes are required not to come on stage except as dress parade arranged between set changes.

Theatre (on stage): Technical rehearsal for setting and lighting (call for stage and electric crews). With the Deputy Stage-Manager and his prompt book fully marked, the Director will first of all check all the circuits to see that they agree with the rig-plot. It is then a matter of going through the entire show checking every scene change and lighting cue, timing the fades, 'builds' and the levels of illumination, watching for light-spills, hot-spots (unwanted concentrations of light) and so on. Part of these proceedings will include the Director requesting someone to walk across stage, with face to the front, so he can test the even spread of illumination.

WEDNESDAY: Theatre: Act One in sets. Full company call. Full technical staff.

THURSDAY: Theatre: Act Two in sets. Full company call as above.

FRIDAY: Theatre: First dress rehearsal. Acts One and Two (as this may be a long rehearsal, an earlier start may be possible). Costumes and make-up. Full technical complement. *Stopping only if necessary. Notes at conclusion.*

SATURDAY: Theatre: Morning call for technical people if required.

SUNDAY: Theatre: Morning call for technical people if required.

Rehearsal Room: Afternoon call for company only if emergency. Otherwise it is better for the company to come to the final dress rehearsal fresh and rested. At the Music Director's discretion an orchestra rehearsal either morning or afternoon, with or without principals, again at his or her discretion.

SUNDAY EVENING: **Final full dress rehearsal.** *As performance.* Full company, orchestra and technical complement. *Curtain up precisely at agreed time* (it could be earlier than public performance time). Interval as performance. *No stopping. Notes at conclusion.*

It should be made clear to all concerned that this rehearsal is to be regarded as a public performance. The Director will have passed on his authority for looking after the performance to the Stage-Manager and the Stage Director (or Deputy Stage-Manager) who will be responsible for starting on time and running the performance in general. In other words, they are on their own. The Director will sit in front, preferably out of obvious sight, with his plots, checking the lighting and stage cues, but unless a dire emergency arises, like the collapse of the scenery or some major catastrophe, will otherwise refrain from going backstage (other than an encouraging brief visit to the working side during the interval) and remain silent and unobtrusive throughout.

At the conclusion, he will have all the company on stage for notes and, if he has done his work thoroughly, these should be brief. In fact, it would be a light-hearted, encouraging few minutes, chiefly occupied by thanking the heads of departments and the company for their patience and co-operation and should certainly end on an up-beat note of 'good luck for the opening night'.

It may be worth noting that there are Directors who regard the dress rehearsals as opportunities to expand their egos by bellowing a stream of instructions to all and sundry in the belief that they are displaying a mastery of technique. In fact what they are doing is showing that they have not done their homework. Bluster is substituted for adequate planning and desk-work. It is not a display of superiority – rather a sign of inadequate technique.

If the circumstances allow the society to organise the fifth week in this manner, with arrangements made with scenic contractors and theatre management, the chances are that the opening night will be mercifully free of the ruinous waits, inexplicable delays and technical contretemps that bedevil the technically under-rehearsed production. It is a much better use of the Director's time (and fee!).

When the situation is not ideal

This usually refers to a four-week rehearsal period as originally described, where the technical work in the theatre has somehow to be squeezed into a matter of hours only on Saturday night (if the venue is a cinema) and Sunday morning, with the technical rehearsal hurried through in the afternoon plus a final dress rehearsal, with the company working in sets in the theatre for the first time. It is in these circumstances that the Director will need to keep his wits about him, control the flow of adrenalin, and be ready with instant solutions to every unexpected crisis.

When pushed for time, it is more than ever desirable to hold a first dress rehearsal on the Friday of the fourth week. And the novice Director should so arrange things that, however pressed, there is time for a technical rehearsal without the actors. Unbelievably, there are (or have been) Directors who lump together the technical rehearsal and the one and only dress rehearsal all in the very last session, which then depressingly goes on for weary hours into the early morning. At such times, when the Stage-Manager has just informed him that the terrace backdrop for Act Two Scene Three is missing and that the French windows they've sent for Scene Five are the wrong height for the flats, and the entire company, technicians and orchestra await to know what he's going to do about it, the last thing the Director will want to know at that juncture is that the maid's bodice is two inches too long and the second male lead's cummerbund is the wrong colour. It is dress rehearsals of this calibre that give rise to the insanely optimistic axiom 'A bad dress rehearsal means a good first night', or that hoary straw clutched at by the hopeful amateur 'It'll be all right on the night'. It may well be – but it shouldn't be relied upon. There are gremlins in the theatre – perhaps even more than anywhere else – who have other ideas.

If and when in such conditions problems arise (as they surely will do), it is the Director who is in the hot seat. His experience and decisiveness will be tested and, in coping with such situations, it is all too easy to make a wrong decision. His greatest ally is time. The wise Director will, therefore, strive not only to circumvent the unexpected with careful planning, but to buy as much time as he can. If he can persuade his producer (the society) of this, both will benefit from that extra fifth week whenever it is possible.

It is in the theatre when, through his planning and efforts, everyone will know what he or she is doing, that the Director will feel the production growing away from him. To a greater and greater extent he will become less and less involved. It is like watching a baby at whose birth he has played a key part, suddenly maturing, standing on its own feet. Now is the time to stand away and let it develop. When the applause comes for a bit of business he has created, there will be (if he is also a performer) a tiny tinge of wistfulness as others take credit for what is his. But overall, there comes the satisfaction of the flowering of artistic creation and – however trite a phrase – of a job well done.

12 | *Lighting Design*

Planning and control

As has already been said, the importance of lighting to a production can scarcely be over-emphasised. In the professional theatre it is now a highly specialised business. A department of its own with its own directors and specialists, who work to interpret the overall ideas of the Director. In so doing they will probably be able to call on a range of lanterns (or luminaires), remote-control focussing, projectors and computerised memory-control panels, for the most part beyond the resources of an amateur society staging a production for one week.

In the limited time available to achieve technical excellence which is often the lot of amateur productions (sometimes one day!), regrettably, lighting is often left to the late inspirations of the Director and the hasty improvisation of amateur Electricians during the dress rehearsal. But lighting is much too important to be left to the last moment. The good Director when planning the sets, changes and staging will, as part of his intuitive grasp, recognise lighting as an integral and major factor contributing to 'flow'.

Five basic requirements

Assuming that in the amateur field the Director is likely to be solely responsible for decisions regarding the final lighting effects, there are five basic requirements necessary to achieve successful results.

1   As part of his art, he should have an understanding of the psychological impact of light and darkness and how their interplay, together with the use of colour, can create and influence mood and atmosphere. If he feels that he does not possess this sensitivity, the only suggestion then would be to make an informed study of pictures, plays and films. Even this may not yield creative results if there is not an innate or intuitive appreciation to begin with. There may not be much more to be said.

2   To give practical expression to his subjective feelings in this respect he must have some knowledge of the instruments, i.e. the lanterns, their uses and limitations, and how they may be linked and controlled. A study of the considerable literature, manufacturers' catalogues and demonstrations can help, but nothing is as effective as actual involvement in their use, i.e. practical experience.

3   He must know what facilities and equipment he will *actually have at his disposal* for any given production. This is where the value of

the questionnaire as shown in Chapter 9, Groundwork, becomes obvious. This should be supplemented by an on-the-spot inspection and a chat with the Electrician concerned.

4   He must have some means of translating the effects he has in mind into a coherent whole, expressed in a language that is understood by those who will be practically interpreting them by mechanical means. In plain terms, this means a lighting design which entails the making of plans showing where light is required, the extent of the area to be covered, what lanterns are to be used, where they are positioned and how they are linked to the correct circuits.

5   He will need some means of charting the use and progress of practical facilities throughout the production in a manner that makes clear the intention and allows ready checking so that control is maintained at every point.

For points 1 and 2, only broad advice may be offered, and point 3 is sufficiently explanatory. Specific proposals are offered in the following pages for the last two requirements.

The lighting rig

Designing the lighting, means first planning the lighting rig. This will be a plan showing the positions of the lighting bars, where on each bar varying types of lanterns are placed, how they are linked to different circuits, and what colours are required. But before starting work on the lighting rig, as mentioned, it is wise to meet the Electrician and together to view the actual installation, lanterns and board and check the accuracy of the replies in the questionnaire.

In particular, now ·is the time to ascertain the precise number of circuits, dimmers and non-dimmers on each bar *that are working and available,* and how they are at present linked to particular lanterns. And what is the maximum loading of each circuit? To overload circuits is to ask for serious trouble. Due to working under pressure of limited time, it is wise to adopt existing layouts and circuit linkages as much as possible, commensurate with the overall scheme.

The rig plot will consist of a plan of each lighting bar showing the positions of each lantern, what type or pattern they are and how they are to be linked to particular circuits. It will help if ¼in squared graph paper is used, preferably of a size big enough to list several bars. Another useful aid is one of those perspex sheets with the shapes of lanterns cut out, so that the outline may be quickly drawn through. Strand Lighting sell them. They come arranged for two scales, 1:25 and

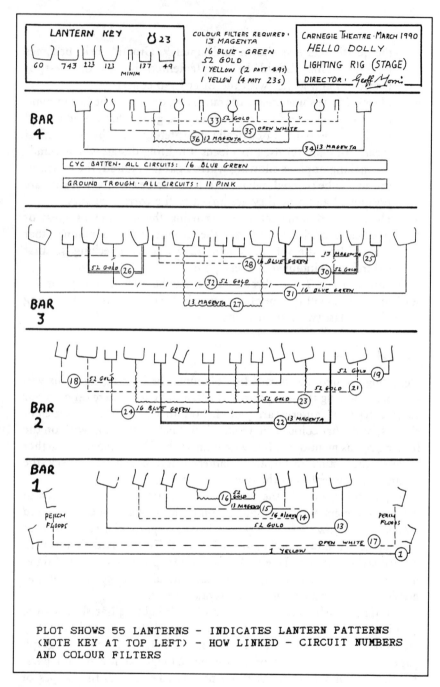

Illustration 16: Part of stage working rig plot

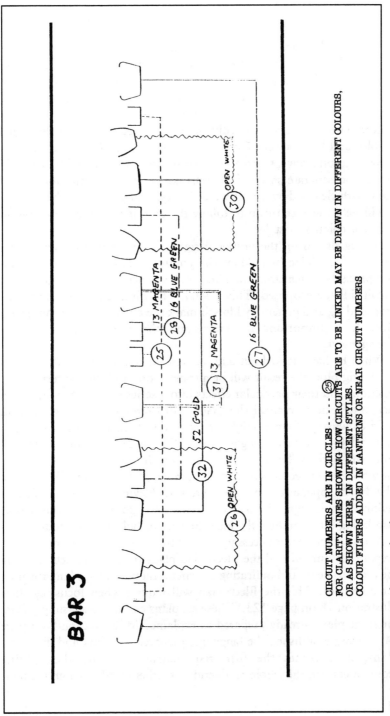

Illustration 17: Circuit diagram detail

1:50. They also incorporate a protractor to calculate beam spread and throw. These may not cater for older lantern patterns. A useful substitute can be one such as students use for geometrical shapes – there is one made for chemistry which is suitable. If such a substitute is used, a lantern key must be shown, identifying the pattern number of the lantern with the shape used. (Illustration 16 page 120 shows the actual rig plot and Illustration 17 on page 121 shows one bar in detail.)

Bars, ground-rows, front-of-house installations should all be similarly drawn, on separate sheets if it seems convenient. The rig plot should show with clearly drawn lines which lanterns are required to be linked – it will help the Electrician to follow the plan if the lines are drawn in different colours or styles.

Having drawn up the proposed rig, it is now time to again confer with the Electrician (who knows his control equipment) and agree with him precisely which circuit numbers on his panel will be allocated to the circuit linkage proposed. This is vital. The Electrician must study the proposed rig and preferably himself mark the circuit numbers on the rig plot. It is important to understand the precise effect of this arrangement.

When he has checked out and marked the number of all the circuits on the rig plot, the result will be a translation of all the lanterns, their positions and their particular effects into a series of circuit numbers. In fact, into a mathematical shorthand. For example: 'Basic lighting, 52 Gold Downstage Centre' might be reduced to Circuit 1; 'Basic lighting, 52 Gold O/P and P/S' might become Circuit 2; 'Mid-stage Centre, 7 Pink' will perhaps be Circuit 7; and so on. In this way the lighting for the whole show becomes a series of numbers, familiar to the Electrician (the board operator) and the Director. Having thus established a definitive language, the Director can now go through the script, translating into numbers the ideas he has for lighting the production.

At this juncture it is necessary, in addition to copies of the rig plot, to prepare for himself and the Electrician plans of the stage sets showing the areas to be lit and indicating the circuit number of the lanterns used for each area. This the Electrician will require when focussing. (See Illustration 18 on page 123.) These set plans can be traced simply from the stage plans already prepared as explained in Illustration 9 on page 84. Having established the language, prepared rig plots and light-area plans, next comes the fifth requirement: charting the lighting requirements for the whole production. In other words the lighting plot.

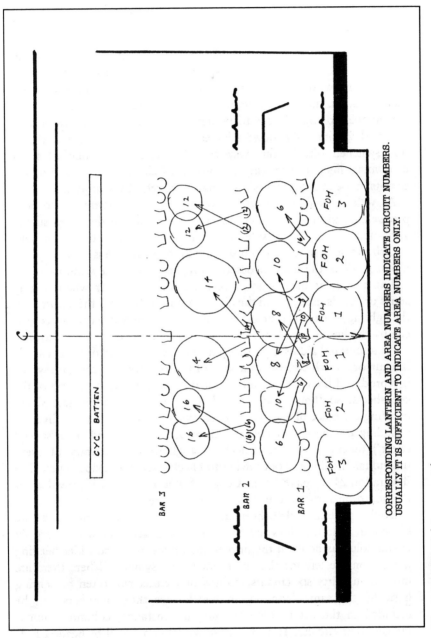

CORRESPONDING LANTERN AND AREA NUMBERS INDICATE CIRCUIT NUMBERS.
USUALLY IT IS SUFFICIENT TO INDICATE AREA NUMBERS ONLY.

Illustration 18: Lighting areas plan

The lighting plot

This has been adapted from an idea put forward in *Tabs*, a quarterly periodical, which Strand Lighting circulated (free) to users of their products a few years ago. Briefly, the idea was to list all the circuit numbers across the paper; then, opposite the cue reference number, to list the numbers of the circuits to be activated, drawing a line from each activated circuit number down the sheet until the cue at which each circuit was switched off. In this way each live circuit was marked by a continuous line, thus making it possible to check the accuracy of the circuits in use at any point without having to refer back to previous cues.

As well as establishing which circuits are in use there has to be a precise indication of how they are to be activated. For this a few simple symbols are placed alongside the cue number. Illustration 19 on page 125 shows the symbols and Illustration 20 on page 126 is an example of a plot made in the manner described together with the symbols.

The particular usefulness of this method, especially where a long series of cues is used, lies in the ability to instantly check the accuracy of the lighting, since every circuit activated is indicated at every subsequent cue by the line. Conversely, if there is no line, the circuit is inactive.

An additional aid used by the author at technical and dress rehearsals is a cursor, which consists of a strip of folded paper, or card, on which is reproduced the circuit numbers lined up with those at the top of the cue sheets, so that it can be slid down each additional cue sheet, marking the place of each cue and showing which circuits are alive. By including on the cursor colour indication, position and (if a 'special effect') function, one can check at a glance the accuracy of every individual circuit, without having to check back to previous cues. (See Illustration 21 on page 127). A copy of plot and cursor is provided for the board operator who usually can work directly from it.

Double foolscap ruled sheets are ideal for plotting. If the sheets are turned so that the lines are vertical, it will accommodate thirty-six circuit columns between the printed blue lines, with the wider heading margin on the left for the cue number and symbol. Where there are more than thirty-six circuits, groups of circuits will often be serving basically the same function, in which case those numbers can be included in the same column; thus, for instance, column 1 might indicate four circuits, 1, 2, 3, and 4, so column 1 will be headed 1–4, and the next column 5 or, if again a group, 5–8. In other circumstances, large squared drawing sheets are available in art shops, giving many more columns.

CUE No.	SYMBOL	MEANS
11		No Symbol : Circuit simply switched on
12	——	"Snap" switch-off
13	∧	"Build" – The addition of a number indicates the time of the build, so
14	/4\ ⌐5	indicates a 4-second build to full or an indicated level, which would also be shown.
15	\2/	Inverted, symbol means Fade. Thus 2-second Fade
16	\/ D·B·O	Fade to Dead Black-Out
17	XF 5	Cross-Fade, i.e., some circuits in, others out in 5 seconds
18	\20/	Deep angle warns of long slow Fade.

Illustration 19: Lighting plot symbols

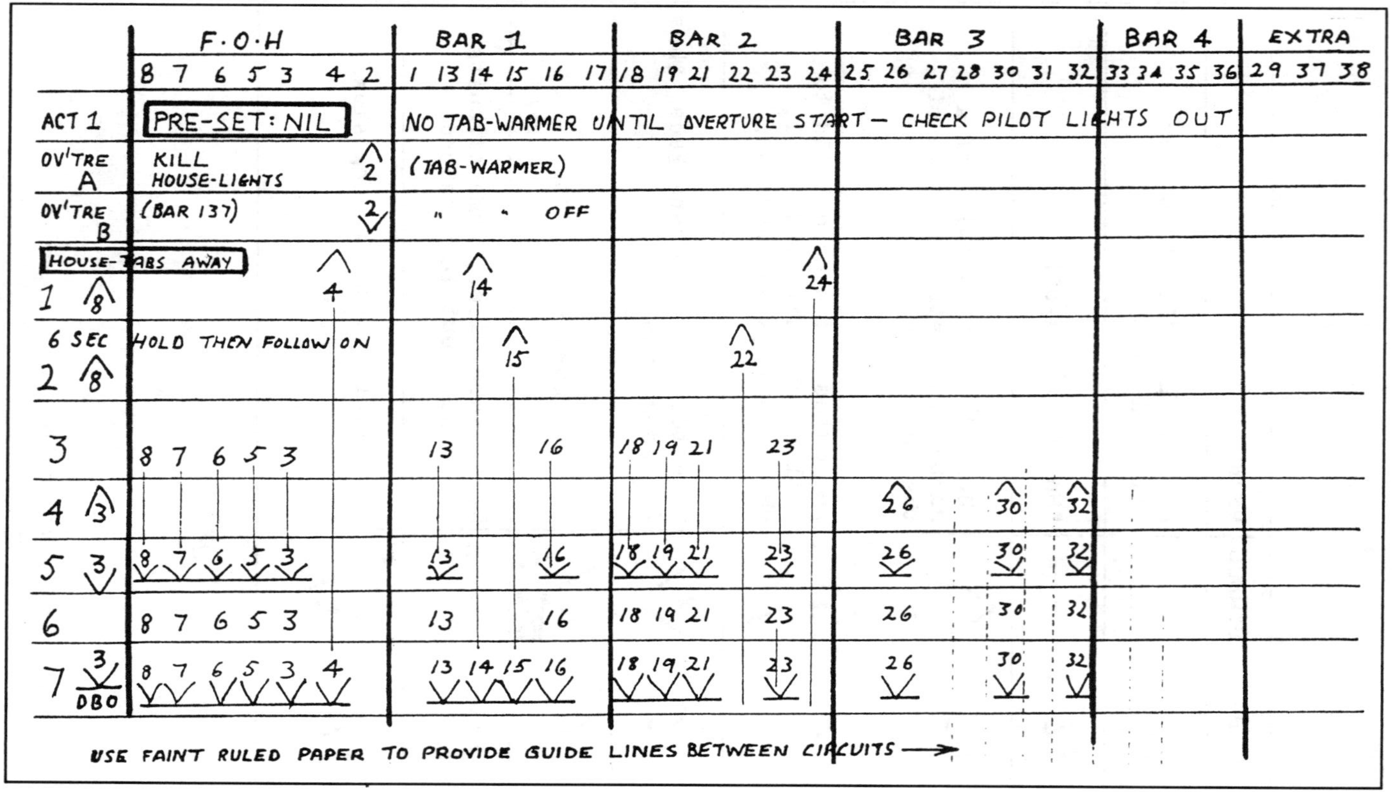

Illustration 20: Lighting plot

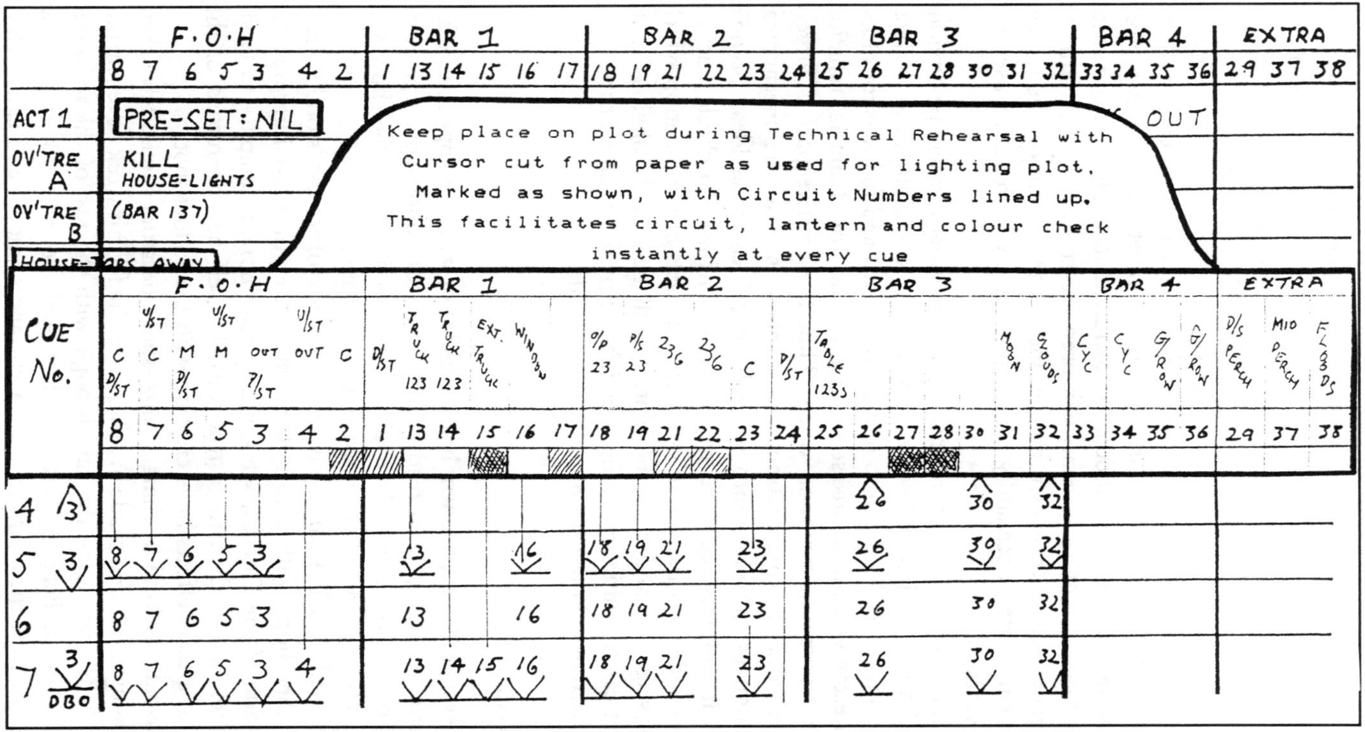
F.O.H
BAR 1
BAR 2
BAR 3
BAR 4
EXTRA
ACT 1
PRE-SET: NIL
OV'TRE A
KILL HOUSE-LIGHTS
OV'TRE B
(BAR 137)
OUT
Keep place on plot during Technical Rehearsal with
Cursor cut from paper as used for lighting plot.
Marked as shown, with Circuit Numbers lined up.
This facilitates circuit, lantern and colour check
instantly at every cue
CUE No.
DBO

Illustration 21: Cursor is instant check during lighting rehearsals

For the sake of clarity and to avoid confusing novice Directors or Designers it may be best to continue to call the supply of electricity to a lantern or group of lanterns a 'circuit'. When the circuit is controlled by a dimmer, it becomes in the prevailing jargon a 'channel'.

The clarity of this method enables constant monitoring of lighting changes with speed and accuracy during rehearsals, welcomed by both amateur and professional board operators. Sometimes the latter, used to their own plotting methods, or fortunate enough to work with boards having memory systems, will prefer to translate the plotting to the requirement of their own boards and systems. That on the whole, the system works successfully can be testified by its repeated use over many years.

From the description of the initial planning stages, it will be obvious that lighting will already have received a great deal of attention. In fact, by the time he settles down to prepare the board and follow-spot plots, the Director will know precisely which circuits (or channels) function for what purpose, how and when. Thus the creative part is largely achieved and the preparation of the plots is now the mechanical translation of the ideas into symbols by which those ideas become reality. In this way technical rehearsal is principally to check that the visualised ideas work, and to establish the levels of illumination which at this stage are added to the plot. It will be equally obvious that, without careful initial planning, the lighting or technical rehearsal can easily become a long drawn out hit-or-miss affair.

Follow-spots

While every other department has some idea of what is happening, with their plots made out and ready to proceed, the follow-spot operators often arrive at the dress rehearsal with no knowledge of the show and completely unprepared. Borrowing a stub of pencil from one another, they hurriedly scribble on the backs of old box-office cards odd words, which they hope will enable them, at a later time, to interpret the inspiration of the Director who, with microphone to amplify to God-like tones his off-the-cuff instructions, himself has no record of the pearls of artistic effects he is creating with the follow-spots.

To avoid this kind of thing, follow-spot operators should have their plots thought out and made in advance of the fourth week of rehearsal, so that when attending the run-through with the rest of the technical people, (see Rehearsal Section) they will be able to familiarise themselves with the characters, their entrances, moves and exits. They will understand the significance of the instructions in the plot, e.g. slow iris in, the use of box-shutter, etc.

Since the follow-spot operators are frequently part-time or casual labour, often unfamiliar with theatrical terminology, or, in the present context, helpers recruited at a late stage, the plot may usefully include in the heading an indication of which side is prompt side and which is opposite prompt. It helps to clearly mark with the letters O/P or P/S and an arrow the side for which the plot is designed – since they will, of course, differ one from the other. A key to explain the symbols and abbreviations used in the plot should be included and the colour filters required listed. The plot is marked in four columns. The first narrow column shows the scene and cue number. The second wider column headed 'Action' indicates briefly what happens on stage. The next, headed 'Focus', tells the operator where and on whom to focus and in what manner. The fourth column tells what colour filter (if any) is required.

The following procedure may be found useful. With the libretto in front, the O/P plot on the left and the P/S on the right, go through the whole show, visualising how, on whom and in what manner the follow-spots will operate, noting the instructions in the four columns, as shown in the reproduction of an actual plot. (See Illustration 22 on page 130). When completed, have them photocopied and explain to the P/S and O/P operators their appropriate copies, retaining the originals for checking during the technical rehearsal.

Follow-spots are an important element in any show and require careful consideration if they are to be effectively used. The method described is well worth the time and trouble involved in preparing the plots, since it will be amply repaid with even more time and trouble avoided at the technical and dress rehearsals.

Guiding principles

Lighting, like much else in the art of directing, is largely subjective. However, there are a few general principles worth considering such as the one that comes first. This is that the actors are more important than the scenery. If the spectators cannot see the protagonists, they may be unable to hear what they are saying, they will not understand what they are doing, and will quickly lose interest, or worse, become irritated, and lose sympathy. Whatever marvellous lighting effects are attempted therefore, the actors must always have priority.

The next most useful guiding principle arises from a consideration of

Workington A.M.Society's
Spring 19—— Production :
PAINT YOUR WAGON

| LIME PLOT | | **P/S** → |

| COLOURS REQUIRED
2 AMBER · 1 YELLOW
17 BLUE · 11 PINK | Up O/P ·

Down O/P | C | Up P/S

Down P/S | WHERE NO COLOUR IS
INDICATED :.
OPEN WHITE |

< IRIS OUT	X OFF
> IRIS IN	>X IRIS IN & OFF
▭ BOX SHUTTER	TRS TRANSFER TO

Scene & Cue No.	ACTION	FOCUS	COLOUR
ACT I **Sc.1** 1	Jennifer discovered O/P	Jennifer	2 AMBER
2	Ben roars with Laughter	>X Jennifer	
INTERLUDE 1	Man enters P/S	Man until EXIT — X	
2	Man enters O/P	Man until EXIT — X	
3	Woman enters P/S	Woman until she is left-alone:- She turns to front and gapes: >X Woman	
Sc 2	STAND BY while Steve and Pete Sing, ready to Focus as soon as they EXIT on :		
1	CHERRY and JAKE C STANDBY UNTIL	< CHERRY and JAKE Follow Jake (smaller IRIS) until EXIT : X	1 YELLOW
2	TWO CHINESE enter up P/S	TWO CHINESE 'Till EXIT : X THEN NIL until Next Scene	

PLOT EXPLAINS SYMBOLS – GIVES CUE NUMBERS – ACTION
ON STAGE – NOW AND ON WHOM TO FOLLOW – AS WELL AS
COLOUR FILTER REQUIRED

Illustration 22: Follow-spot plot

the function of the eye itself. The eye naturally focusses on the point of attention (i.e. the action, be it actual movement or development of plot), while the periphery of vision remains slightly out of focus. Accordingly, the light should, as it were, target downstage centre and spread out to encompass the rest of the stage in accordance with the action and requirements of the scene.

If, as frequently, there are a limited number of lanterns, the first concern is that there should be an agreeably bright basic spread of light from downstage to at least two thirds of the distance upstage. This is almost invariably the area where most of the action will occur, so it is important that it be well lit. (In theory, upstage centre, from a purely dramatic viewpoint, is the dominant position. In practice, when dealing with musicals, it will be found that for reasons arising from sight-lines coupled with positions of ensemble groupings, unless rostra are involved, it is more expedient to bring important action somewhere about mid-stage.)

The centre of the stage is not only the area where the spectator's eye tends to focus and where most of the action will take place, it is also the area further from lanterns either side-stage or front of house and, therefore, if not given special consideration can easily become a relatively dark area. To avoid this, in-stage lighting areas may to some extent be overlapped so as to ensure a strong saturation there. The last third – upstage area – must not, of course, be neglected. One must ensure that it is all covered with the basic lighting, but if resources are slender, in accordance with the principles mentioned, allow a greater saturation downstage.

Again, if lighting facilities are limited, overspill from the important acting areas may be sufficient to light the scenery, though this cannot be elevated to a hard and fast rule since there are many occasions when backcloths, or other special areas, will require to be lit – perhaps with filtered light to boost colour effects. A blue cyclorama, for instance, will require a good many lanterns, generally including a cyclorama batten and a ground trough or a batten of pattern 49 Floods to achieve an even saturation of blue light. Incidentally, if a blue stage is required, it will take a lot more lanterns to achieve an even, effective blue saturation than is required for other lighter colours. This is where magazine battens can play a very useful part, especially if they are sectionalised, allowing parts of them to be used.

Scenic backdrops can be a problem. If they are not evenly lit, perspective can be lost and their effectiveness ruined. A cloth too near a spot batten may, by the uneven distribution of light, lose much of its effectiveness with spills of light from spotlights destroying any pretensions if may have had in contributing to an overall stage picture. Where resources are limited and no magazine battens available, better let cloths be lit by overspill from acting areas and subsidiary throw from front-of-house spots.

Side lighting can lend depth to a scene and be a very useful adjunct to exteriors which are to be visible from interior sets, e.g. a view of the garden through the window or the light from outside when an exterior door is to be opened. It is also of particular effectiveness in full ensemble scenes. Skilful use of side lighting to highlight crowd scenes can lend depth and dramatic perspective.

Downstage front-cloth scenes need careful lighting. If there is a spot-bar nearby, there is always a risk that unsightly hot-spots will not only ruin any scenic purpose the cloth may have had, but also distract the eye of the spectator from the performer. Barn-doors, to limit the light-spread, can be brought into use, but these can also limit the usefulness of a lantern whose primary purpose is for an upstage area. A satisfactory solution is often to use the front-of-house soft area Fresnels used for downstage and mid-centre areas, which will tend to make a pool of light about three-quarters up the cloth, allowing the top quarter to gently fade. In this way it will be in consonance with the natural behaviour of the eye as it focusses on the central area of activity.

The Director will not neglect the use of darkness itself. It can be used as an equivalent of the cinema close-up, i.e. with a spotlight to isolate a character temporarily from his or her surroundings – providing it is used with discretion and judgement. One example would be the trio for Adam, Millie and Gideon from *Seven Brides For Seven Brothers* where each expresses his or her own line of thought, isolated from each other by being lit by individual spotlights in surrounding darkness. Where a change of scene can be done quickly, and where there is no front-cloth action to cover, rather than closing the No 1 runners, putting up the lights, then opening the curtains, a blackout seems to add to the pace and flow.

It always looks messy and ill-conceived to allow front-of-house spots, which form part of the lighting of a scene, to impinge on curtains before they part to disclose that scene. The eye will be distracted by irrelevant patches of light and the surprise element of the next scene will be weakened.

A scene that is intended to be dimly lit as part of the dramatic situation if darkened too long can be wearying for the spectator. The solution is to commence the scene at a low level of illumination to establish the atmosphere then, after a minute or so, to increase the level gradually, in a slow build of about forty to sixty seconds, to a more acceptable level. This, again, is in accord with the natural function of the eye which adapts to available light. We are simply helping it a little to make sure no action is missed. Towards the end of the scene, the level of illumination may be dropped – slightly faster – unless, as is probable, there is a dramatic finish to the scene. In which case a fade to blackout is the preferred ploy.

The use of colour filters will depend upon the facilities available and the Director's approach. However, a couple of hints may be offered. For basic lighting, Strand Lighting 52 Gold is a sound choice. It is warmer than the oft-used straws, and lends itself to pancake make-up, often favoured these days. For night scenes where there are only moderate lantern facilities, Strand Lighting 16 Blue-Green may be found useful. It is bright enough, at full strength, to suggest moonlight and can, of course, be darkened by lowering the level of the dimmers. Used in conjunction with 32 Blue on the cyclorama it can be very effective.

13 | *Flow*

Ideas for quick scene changes

Presentation

For quite valid artistic and/or economic reasons there is a contemporary tendency to keep scenic settings as simple as possible. While the intellectual force of a drama may be conveyed adequately, even reinforced, by a spartan setting of a plain cyclorama, rostra, treads and a few chairs, the emotional appeal of a musical will be that much lessened without some degree of spectacle. Where music, song and dance are important ingredients, the success of a story so constructed and conveyed will be immeasurably enhanced by a succession of colourfully-lit settings. In this context, therefore, scenery, setting and changes are important.

The older type of musical often followed a pattern in which full stage sets regularly alternated with front cloth scenes giving time for set changes. The frequent 'scene-change music' appearing in scores is evidence of the long waits endured by the audience, staring (not always patiently) at the No 1 runners while stage-hands bumped and thumped scenery and props behind. Even in comparatively recent scores 'scene-change music' is still to be found.

In more contemporary times, directors and designers of original productions use all the resources of modern stagecraft to eliminate scene-change waits. For example, *Paint Your Wagon* with eighteen scenes designed to follow one another non-stop, or *Hello Dolly* with fifteen scenes through which characters walk and continue the dialogue while the scenes change around them without a break.

If a production of this nature is contemplated in venues somewhat lacking in facilities, and reliance is placed on older and conventional methods of presentation, it will soon become obvious that these will prove quite inadequate to ensure a pace and impact anywhere approaching that of the original.

Some scenic contractors, having bought the scenery from the original professional resident or touring production, will hire it to those amateur societies able to stage their productions in professional theatres, in which case the Director will have the use of the original settings and equipment. Other scenic contractors will contrive to match the sets (often in two or more sizes), sometimes using older sets from other productions refurbished to fit. What is then offered to the amateur society may be an approximation of the original but lacking much of its technical innovation.

In some respects this becomes a self-perpetuating situation where contractors have to supply scenery for use on stages they know to be inadequately equipped, and societies continue to use what is supplied because there may be a lack of knowledge or impetus to explore new or different methods to overcome poor facilities. Contractors are frequently quite willing to co-operate with the staging ideas of Directors provided they are sound and adequately designed. Sometimes it is a matter of imbuing the society's Stage-Manager, his committee and helpers with the enthusiasm to physically construct items adapted to local conditions and augment what is supplied by the contractor.

Making the show run smoothly

There is much that can be done in the field of amateur productions to ensure good flow and presentation given the will and drive to achieve it. After all, one feels that if Senor Torelli de Fano (reputed to be the first man to use mobile scenery) could change one full set to another in about twenty seconds, using what must have been somewhat primitive methods in Venice over three hundred years ago, it should be possible, emulating his pioneering spirit, and with a little knowledge of the technical know-how available nowadays, for even amateur societies to do something to improve the speed of changes. Some suggestions are offered here; all have actually been put into practice in the past. If they prove useful, or if they spark off other ideas for improvements, so much the better.

Flying

There is probably no faster method of changing scenery than by simply 'flying', i.e. raising or lowering it with ropes and pulleys set in a 'grid' above the stage. Problems arise when there is insufficient height above the borders to lift the whole depth of a cloth out of sight. However, there are ways in which the difficulty may be overcome.

Cloth clips

A backcloth is usually battened out, and the top batten tied to the ropes which will raise it to the grid. If the height required to fly it out of sight above the borders is insufficient by only a few feet it may still be possible to fly the cloth by using cloth clips. Instead of tying the ropes to the batten at the top of the cloth, they are tied to cloth clips, which are shaped metal hooks. By rolling the cloth around the top batten as many times as required, the overall height of the cloth can be reduced. The top batten, with the cloth so rolled, can then have the cloth clips slid on, the clips tied to the lines and so flown and deaded as usual. Of course there is a limit to the amount by which the top of the cloth may be so reduced, depending upon the design, and height of the borders.

At one cinema venue, however, by lowering the borders two feet and using cloth clips it proved possible to fly cloths where for years previously they had persisted with hand-rolling for every scene change. At other places where lack of height above the stage made hand-rolling of the backdrops the usual practice, unnecessary waits caused by this problem were obviated by the method of 'triple-hitch flying'.

Triple-hitch flying

The cloth is suspended from a batten in the usual way and after being 'deaded' is tied off. The batten on the set of lines immediately behind is then attached to the back of the cloth at a convenient height with webbing or strong tapes and safety-pins. This becomes a 'hitch-batten' and it is this batten which is pulled up to raise the cloth. In so doing, it effectively folds the cloth into three 'drops' thus enabling it to be flown out of sight in a third of the space it would normally require if pulled up 'straight'. (See Illustration 23 on page 137). In a theatre where the bottom edge of the borders were 12ft above stage level with only 9ft above this to the grid, by using this device with the hitch-batten set at 6ft up from stage level, it proved possible to fly an 18ft cloth. This method is more adaptable to lighter aniline-dye type cloths and is probably not suitable for heavily painted canvas backdrops.

Roll and tumble

Then there is 'roll and tumble'. In this procedure, the cloth is hung in the usual way, then the bottom batten of the cloth is tied to the set of lines immediately behind, so that it is suspended both top and bottom. The cloth is then raised a few inches from the bottom and a roller wooden batten (or similar metal tubing), the same width as the cloth, is put in along the bottom of the fold. It is then deaded to stage level. The cloth is flown by pulling up both top and bottom battens, and, when raised above the borders, only occupies half its normal depth.

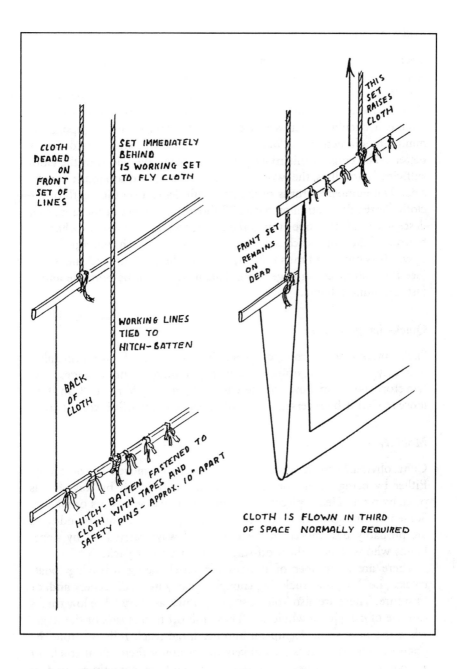

CLOTH DEADED ON FRONT SET OF LINES

SET IMMEDIATELY BEHIND IS WORKING SET TO FLY CLOTH

WORKING LINES TIED TO HITCH-BATTEN

BACK OF CLOTH

HITCH-BATTEN FASTENED TO CLOTH WITH TAPES AND SAFETY PINS - APPROX. 10" APART

THIS SET RAISES CLOTH

FRONT SET REMAINS ON DEAD

CLOTH IS FLOWN IN THIRD OF SPACE NORMALLY REQUIRED

Illustration 23: Triple-hitch flying

Roller cloths

There is another method (sometimes misnamed 'roll and tumble') which is widely used in smaller theatres. This consists of rolling the cloths from the bottom upwards with ropes and pulleys. Here the top of the cloth is fixed to a stationary batten, while the bottom is wrapped around a circular roller which can be of wood or metal piping. (A minimum diameter of 2½in is recommended, though up to 5in is better.) The ends of this roller protrude beyond the width of the cloth sufficiently to allow the 'working lines' to be wound around it at each side. The number of turns of the rope will depend on the depth of the cloth. As the illustration on page 139 shows, the weight of the cloth as it descends winds the rope around the roller, so it is fully wound when the bottom of the cloth reaches the stage. To raise the cloth, the rope pulled upwards is unwound thus in turn, winding the cloth around the roller. (See Illustration 24 on page 139). This method can be portable and is fast and quite reliable.

Quick-change scenery

Slick smooth scene changes generally make use of two principles: 'mobility' and 'reversibility'. When planning scene changes, the Director, intent on flow will be constantly asking himself: 'Can it be moved? Can it be reversed?' Very often the answer will involve both.

Mobility

Quite obviously most scenery is designed to be moved in some way. Either by being flown, or dismantled and carried off by stage-hands piece by piece. Heavy pieces can be built to move on castors or wheels. Sometimes tracks or rails are used. Lighter pieces such as ground-rows are probably best moved in the traditional way: carried off by stage-hands who will store them off-stage in their correct pack.

There are a number of devices for set-changing involving 'boat-trucks', i.e. low, flat trucks big enough to carry items of scenery and/or furniture. There are also 'rolling stages', which are very large low trucks capable of carrying a whole set. These roll off to one side of the stage, while the next scene set up on another large truck rolls on from the opposite side. Amateurs are unlikely to encounter them. Boat-trucks of various sizes undoubtedly speed changes and are sometimes used in amateur productions, but are often ruled out by the lack of off-stage

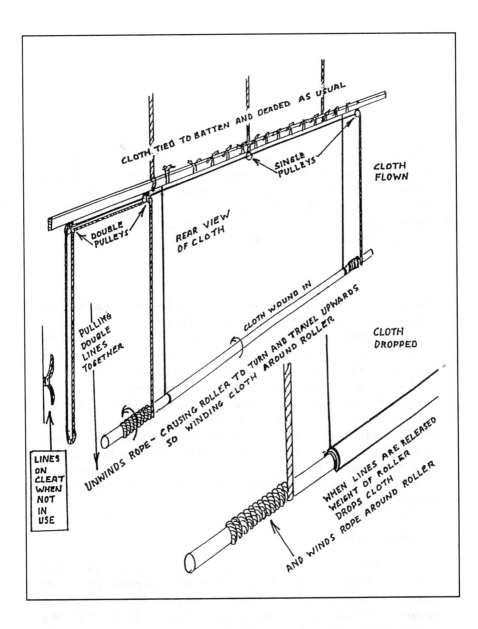

CLOTH TIED TO BATTEN AND DEADED AS USUAL

SINGLE PULLEYS

CLOTH FLOWN

DOUBLE PULLEYS

REAR VIEW OF CLOTH

PULLING DOUBLE LINES TOGETHER

CLOTH WOUND IN

CLOTH DROPPED

UNWINDS ROPE – CAUSING ROLLER TO TURN AND TRAVEL UPWARDS SO WINDING CLOTH AROUND ROLLER

LINES ON CLEAT WHEN NOT IN USE

WHEN LINES ARE RELEASED WEIGHT OF ROLLER DROPS CLOTH AND WINDS ROPE AROUND ROLLER

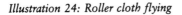

Illustration 24: Roller cloth flying

space. Perhaps for the generality of amateur productions desiring to promote flow, the principle most often involved is that of reversibility.

Reversibility

Reversibility quite simply means turning something, a piece of scenery, a flat or truck, around to show its other side. The advantage becomes immediately apparent when it is realised that, to start with, it doesn't have to be carried off-stage and something else brought on to replace it, that it can be done very quickly on the spot, and very probably without drawing the curtain or blacking out. All of which adds up to speed and flow. An obvious example is the use of flippers.

Flippers

These are pieces of scenery painted on both sides and hinged to other flats, and when turned on their hinges, rather like the pages of a book, reveal their obverse side, and at the same time disclose the portion of the flat which they have been covering. A glance at the folder wing-piece (or book-wing) will show the idea (see Illustration 25 on page 141).

This principle is particularly useful in productions with a standing set in which the action takes place in selected areas (like *Oliver*, where the use of a large revolve is not possible). Used in conjunction with one or two reversible pieces it can be extremely effective where a scene has to be repeated. It will be obvious that pieces of scenery to be reversible, must be painted on both sides and, therefore, as far as possible, free-standing, i.e. not requiring braces and weights, which leads on to reversible trucks.

Reversible trucks

A free-standing truck on castors can be constructed and painted on both sides, perhaps with an additional flipper, so as to represent two or more quite different objects. For example (again from *Oliver*) a fireplace complete with hanging cauldron, central to Fagin's kitchen, built on a reversible truck, with a 12in flipper raised on top, became a fruit stall. Together with two other similar trucks, the whole scene was changed to the Street Market scene in approximately five seconds. Reversible trucks naturally lead to the complete revolve.

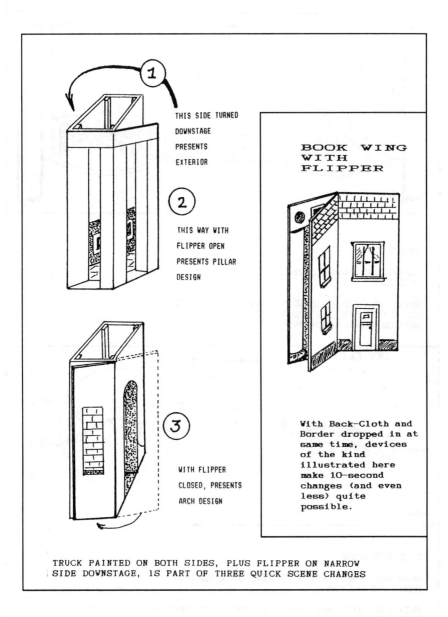

① THIS SIDE TURNED DOWNSTAGE PRESENTS EXTERIOR

② THIS WAY WITH FLIPPER OPEN PRESENTS PILLAR DESIGN

③ WITH FLIPPER CLOSED, PRESENTS ARCH DESIGN

BOOK WING
WITH
FLIPPER

With Back-Cloth and Border dropped in at same time, devices of the kind illustrated here make 10-second changes (and even less) quite possible.

TRUCK PAINTED ON BOTH SIDES, PLUS FLIPPER ON NARROW SIDE DOWNSTAGE, IS PART OF THREE QUICK SCENE CHANGES

Illustration 25: Quick-change scenery

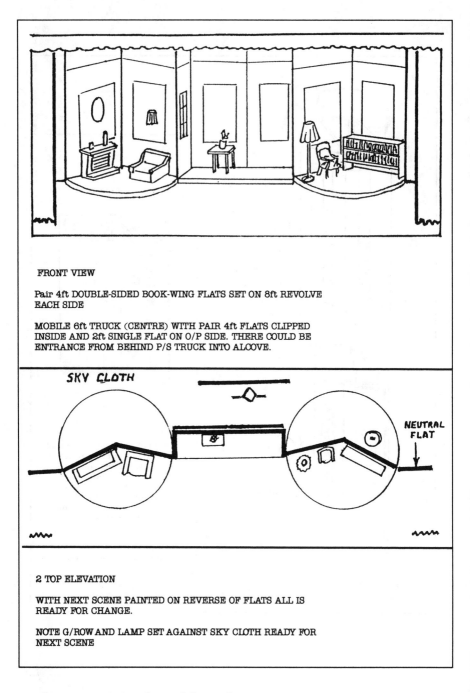

FRONT VIEW

Pair 4ft DOUBLE-SIDED BOOK-WING FLATS SET ON 8ft REVOLVE
EACH SIDE

MOBILE 6ft TRUCK (CENTRE) WITH PAIR 4ft FLATS CLIPPED
INSIDE AND 2ft SINGLE FLAT ON O/P SIDE. THERE COULD BE
ENTRANCE FROM BEHIND P/S TRUCK INTO ALCOVE.

SKY CLOTH

NEUTRAL
FLAT

2 TOP ELEVATION

WITH NEXT SCENE PAINTED ON REVERSE OF FLATS ALL IS
READY FOR CHANGE.

NOTE G/ROW AND LAMP SET AGAINST SKY CLOTH READY FOR
NEXT SCENE

Illustration 26A: Revolves and flat truck

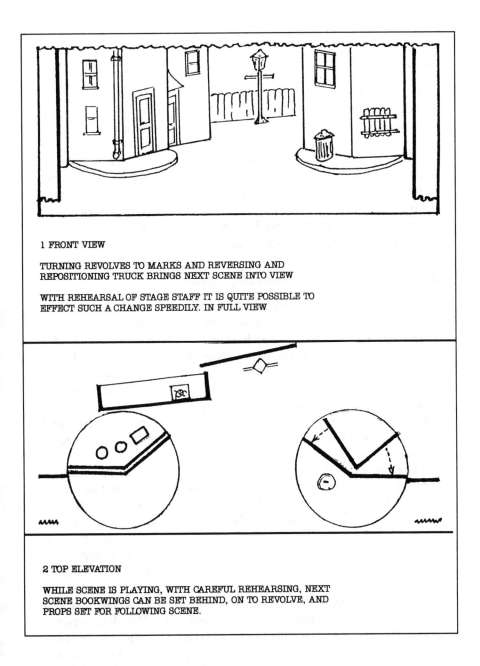

1 FRONT VIEW

TURNING REVOLVES TO MARKS AND REVERSING AND
REPOSITIONING TRUCK BRINGS NEXT SCENE INTO VIEW

WITH REHEARSAL OF STAGE STAFF IT IS QUITE POSSIBLE TO
EFFECT SUCH A CHANGE SPEEDILY. IN FULL VIEW

2 TOP ELEVATION

WHILE SCENE IS PLAYING, WITH CAREFUL REHEARSING, NEXT
SCENE BOOKWINGS CAN BE SET BEHIND, ON TO REVOLVE, AND
PROPS SET FOR FOLLOWING SCENE.

Illustration 26B: Revolves and flats truck scene change

The revolving stage

The revolving stage is of great use particularly in plays involving a number of complete changes of sets including furniture. One scene can be playing before the audience while the following scene in its entirety, including furniture, built pieces, lighting and so forth, is set behind. An excellent facility making for some spectacular scenic effects, but out of reach of most amateur societies, in all probability, unless they are able to produce in top-class professional theatres. If a revolve seems beyond the possibility of the average society, the advantages of such a facility to a considerable extent may still be available by the perhaps surprising expedient of having three revolves instead!

A permanent, adaptable quick-change scheme

The idea presented here is based on a system which has proved highly successful in a number of productions making use of both principles: reversibility and mobility. It has been used with amateur groups who have made their own scenery to the author's design, and also adapted for use with scenery as supplied by contractors. As outlined here it is based on the use of standard 4ft wide flats, both singly and hinged to make book-wings. No extensive knowledge of mechanical or electrical engineering is required, just a moderate degree of commonsense and stage-sense. What *is* required is a resourceful Stage-Manager and some willing helpers.

The scheme proposed consists of two revolving platforms pivoted one each side of the stage, plus a mobile truck, not anchored, but able to be reversed and/or moved to any required position. The precise positions of the two revolves will depend on the dimensions of the stage, and how far up from the setting line it will be most convenient to place them. It may be quite possible to arrange two different positions, depending upon the requirements of the production, though it is unlikely that their situations will change during the same production.

The dimensions offered here are suitable for a stage with a proscenium opening somewhere in the region of 24ft. Each revolve will be 8ft in diameter, and the truck will be 8ft 3½in wide, and not less than 2ft 3½in deep. Depending on the depth of the acting area, the depth of the truck may be extended to 3ft 4in, or best of all to 4ft 3½in, thus allowing it to make use of 4ft flats on its narrower sides. In use it will reveal either a closed side, or an open interior, useful for entrances, alcoves, corridors or whatever may be required. In Illustration 26A on page 142, it can be seen as an alcove with an entrance on the prompt side. Illustration 26B on page 143 shows the front view and top elevation of an exterior scene.

Simple revolves

Each revolve is made of 25mm blockboard, 8ft in diameter (this will require two sheets of blockboard 8ft x 4ft for each revolve). A minimum of four bearers 75mm x 38mm screwed to the underside are set at right angles to the blockboard filling, as shown in the illustration on page 146. Six 4in solid rubber or rubber-tyred, swivel castors are fixed 8in from the edge on the bearers (see Illustration 27 on page 146). In the exact centre of the revolve a 30mm hole is bored and through this is dropped a length of steel barrelling or pipe with a flange to prevent it dropping through. This forms the pivot on which the structure turns.

When the revolve has been placed in the required position, a 30mm hole is bored (through the hole of the revolve) down into the stage and the pivot dropped into position. It will be found that the revolve turns easily with this arrangement.

There is then the problem when repositioning the revolve after it has been removed, of finding the hole in the stage again. This is solved in the following way. With the revolve in the correct position on its pivot (and all this should be done the first time the pivot is placed through the revolve into the hole in the stage), make a permanent mark at the edge of the revolve, preferably upstage. Make a mark on the stage to correspond with the mark on the platform of the revolve. At a quarter of the circumference from the first mark, make a second mark on the edge of the revolve and a corresponding mark on the stage. Thus when the revolve is to be positioned, if the marks on the revolve are lined up with the marks on the stage, the pivot hole in revolve and stage will correspond, and the pivot easily dropped into position. A second revolve is constructed and placed in the corresponding position on the other side of the stage.

The precise positions are best determined when flats are in situation on the revolve, since the off-stage flat should just clear the edge of the wing-piece standing on stage (or neutral leg) so as to mask. When the scene is changed, if necessary, the masking wings or legs (or neutral tabs) can be inched instage to join the flat on the revolve. (See Illustration 26B, Top Elevation, on page 143).

Each revolve should have a 6in canvas 'skirt' tacked around the edge to hide the castors. Even when carrying built pieces, with a raised

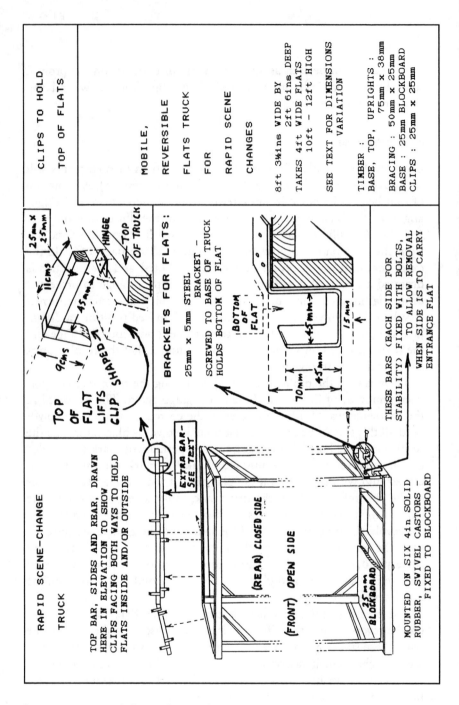

Illustration 27: Rapid change flats truck

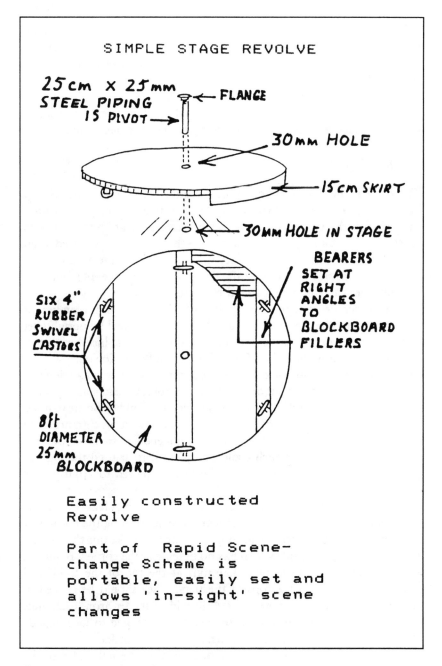

SIMPLE STAGE REVOLVE

25cm x 25mm STEEL PIPING IS PIVOT

FLANGE

30mm HOLE

15cm SKIRT

30mm HOLE IN STAGE

BEARERS SET AT RIGHT ANGLES TO BLOCKBOARD FILLERS

SIX 4" RUBBER SWIVEL CASTORS

8ft DIAMETER 25mm BLOCKBOARD

Easily constructed Revolve

Part of Rapid Scene-change Scheme is portable, easily set and allows 'in-sight' scene changes

Illustration 28: Simple revolve construction

balcony or rostrums, it will be found that the whole thing turns quite easily and smoothly. Should the stage be badly worn where the revolve is to operate, it is quite possible to nail down strips of hardboard to smooth the passage of the castors.

In removing the revolve, the pivot is lifted out by its flange, the revolve up-ended on to its edge and wheeled off-stage taking only a few inches of space in the scenic pack, ready for use the next time.

Quick-change flats truck

The truck is the third component of the quick-change scheme. As will be seen from Illustration 26A on page 142, it takes the central position to join with the two revolves. It can be set either, as shown with its 'open' position forming part of the set – in this instance, visualised as an alcove with an entrance on the prompt side (behind the prompt side revolve); or, as in Illustration 26B, Front View, on page 143, with its 'closed' side, carrying flats painted to represent a street scene.

It is of simple construction. Built with 75mm x 38mm timber, it consists of a rectangular base and an identical top, joined by uprights set into the inside corners of the bottom and top. The base has three cross-members to help support the 25mm blockboard floor. The narrow sides may be braced with 50mm x 25mm cross-members, set at an angle from the top to approximately 5ft down. At the bottom, to lend stability a bar can be bolted across with bolts and wing-nuts. It should be borne in mind that either of the narrow ends may require to be used as an entrance. The brace at the top, therefore, should be high enough to be above the opening in a door-flat, which could be up to 6½ft. If used thus for an entrance, the bar at the bottom can be easily removed to avoid people tripping over it.

For the sake of stability, the truck needs bracing on at least one of the large sides. In the illustration, braces are seen supporting the corners at the (rear) side. To conceal them, it is necessary to make this the 'closed' side, while the (front) side which has no bracing at the corners requiring concealment is the 'open' side. The rails at the top of the truck will require 'clips' to hold the tops of the flats. They should be spaced in pairs 40in apart, so as to hold the 48in wide flats 4in from each end. There should be four clips (two for each flat) arranged to face outside the truck, and four clips similarly arranged to face inside.

Using timber of the dimensions indicated, the external width of the truck at 8ft 3½in is sufficient to allow a pair of 4ft flats to be clipped inside the top side-rails of the truck allowing ½in play to cope with any variation in the size of the flats. In this position, clipped at the top and resting on the floor of the truck, they form the backing to the open side (see Illustration 26B, Front View, on page 143).

Another pair of 4ft flats can be clipped to the outside of the closed side, with the bottoms of the flats carried in steel brackets. In other words, one set of flats facing downstage show an interior, and backing them is another set facing upstage, ready when the truck is turned to be part of the next scene. Note however that allowing for 4ft flats inside and also allowing for the 1½in truck corner uprights, the external width will be 3in wider than the two 4ft flats on the outside. This 3in gap, however, can easily be concealed by setting the side where the gap occurs behind the edge of the off-stage matching flat or drape.

The truck illustration on page 146 shows the top rails of the truck with the clips spaced out and facing both ways. The 'extra bar' indicated is simply a length of timber set between the uprights and attached to the rear bar on the inside to make a level surface to support the inside flats between the two narrow side rails.

Clips

These are shown in detail in the illustration on page 146. Made from 25mm square timber, they are hinged to the top rail. Allow 1¾in (45mm) between the rail and the shaped piece. This gives a little play, should there be any variation in the thickness of the flats. The shaped surface, as shown, makes it easy to steer the top of the flat into the clip. In use, the flat is lifted up into the clip, and dropped into the steel brackets along the bottom rails. (When facing inwards, the flats simply rest on the blockboard).

Brackets

These need little explanation beyond the detailed drawing shown on page 146. They are simple steel brackets which should be fixed in a position corresponding to the clips at the top. There should be four along the outside of the closed side, and two each on the outside of the narrow sides.

Dimensions

Precise dimensions will depend upon the size of the stage. Those proposed here envisage the use of standard size 4ft flats. The scheme would be suitable for a proscenium opening of between 20 and 24ft and even a little wider, with judicious use of neutral tabs, legs or portals.

The height to the top of the truck is not indicated, since this will depend upon the height at which borders are normally set and the height of flats normally used. 10 and 12ft are convenient sizes, and 14ft flats may be possible. The height of the revolves and base of the truck will add perhaps 6in or so to the overall height. It may be borne in mind that with careful lighting, following the principle already stated (i.e. the natural focussing of the eye), the tops of the flats may merge into darkness, allowing the borders to be set barely touching the flats, so as not to impede movement of trucks or revolves in quick repositioning.

What is most important is that the height of the flats to be used must be equalled by the distance between the top clips in their closed position and brackets at the bottom. 4ft book-wings can be used on the truck either inside or outside, as well as single 4ft flats.

The depth of the truck is also optional depending upon off-stage space. Ideally it should be no less than 2ft 3½in, so as to allow it to be used as an alcove, or an interior with an entrance. And that is about the minimum required depth for someone to walk through with ease. This size also allows a little play for a 2ft flat to be inserted and clipped on the interior. Again, ideally, it would be 4ft in depth, to take a 4ft flat on the narrow sides. It all depends upon how much space there is to store it off-stage when not required. It may also be mentioned that when clipped in position the flats themselves will lend stability to the structure.

Flats for the revolve

These should be 4ft book-wings, which will stand by themselves. This allows a second pair of book-wings to be added upstage, while the scene is playing downstage as indicated in Illustration 26B, Top Elevation, on page 143. Or, as suggested, they could be reversible, i.e. painted on both sides.

Scenic effects

It will be obvious that in-depth scenic structures can be built on the revolve, with entrances, balconies and windows possible for the Designer with ingenuity. (Used in *The White Horse Inn*, for instance, one showed the entrance to the Inn with double doors at stage level, and balcony above, and while reversed it showed an interior with an upper 'practical' level. The opposite revolve displayed an Alpine House with door at stage level and practical upper-level window, with shutters, and firm enough to accommodate three of the cast. On the obverse side, it managed a raised entrance to match an interior.)

This scheme, using the two revolves, and a variation of the truck idea (i.e. sometimes two similar trucks on similar lines), were used most successfully for a number of productions, usually those requiring rapid scene changes without breaks, like *Hello Dolly*, *Paint Your Wagon*, *My Fair Lady*, and *Calamity Kate*.

Societies and amateur groups who stage their productions in the limiting circumstances of inadequately equipped stages may find the ideas and suggestions offered in this chapter helpful. If not adopted in their entirety, they may nevertheless stimulate other ideas and methods more suitable to their own particular needs. Should this be the case they are likely to find a great deal of artistic satisfaction in exploring new avenues of presentation.

For the Director, there is nothing quite so satisfying as seeing the production flowing smoothly, one scene dissolving kaleidoscopically into the next, without break or interruption. That should be his goal. However, it should be emphasised that the scene change should never be featured for itself. It must take place unobtrusively and effortlessly as an adjunct to the players as they present the story.

The rapid scene change done in sight during exits or entrances will, of course, mean a great deal more work for him, both in the initial scenic and lighting planning. Very often it will necessitate the devising of extra choreographic movement downstage, or movement for principal characters, while the scene changes around them. While stage technicians moving trucks, flats, etc., will keep out of sight, players may sometimes, to a limited extent, be involved in assisting the scene change, perhaps by moving a prop or small piece upstage, or turning a free-standing truck. This may be explained (even rehearsed with chairs, or similar items) in the rehearsal room to the players, but will require careful rehearsal with players and stage staff in the actual set on stage.

The Director, who retains a love of the theatre and regards it as a realm where wonder and enchantment still find a natural place, will doubtless regard the extra work, care and attention well worthwhile if he can add a touch of magic to his stagecraft.

14 | *And in Addition*

The Director's other concerns

As well as his efforts in the rehearsal room each evening, and his preoccupation with staging, rig and lighting plots during the day, the Director will find other matters ancillary to his main task of bringing the production to life. Some of them are briefly considered here.

Wardrobe

The usual arrangement is that the costumes for the whole production are hired from a firm specialising in theatrical wardrobe. Usually, also, this important department is in the control of the society Wardrobe Mistress, who generally has a number of assistants to help. As a rule, preliminary arrangements with the suppliers and the taking of measurements from all those requiring costumes will have been taken care of before the Director arrives on the scene, though in special circumstances he may have been consulted at an earlier date.

It is usual for the Director to have a copy of the wardrobe plot as proposed by the suppliers at an early date, so he can raise any queries in good time. For some productions where no established wardrobe is available, say for a revue or a pantomime, the Director will almost certainly be called upon to devise the wardrobe plot himself – especially if he intends to introduce some novelty. This he will have to attend to early in the proceedings if costumes have to be designed and made to measure.

Wherever possible, if should be arranged for costumes to be supplied at as early a date as can be agreed. If, as suggested here, the first dress rehearsal is scheduled for the Friday before the Monday opening, the costumes will need to be delivered and taken to the rehearsal room as soon as possible so that the Wardrobe Mistress can unpack before rehearsal commences. If as also suggested, a fifth week of rehearsal is possible, costumes should arrive on the Monday or Tuesday of that week, so that a wardrobe call can be arranged in the dressing rooms of the theatre on Tuesday evening. Dress parades can be arranged between set changes during the technical rehearsal.

If favourable business arrangements exist between the society and the suppliers, it is not at all uncommon for the suppliers when told of rehearsal arrangements to be willing to send costumes at an earlier date, especially if they are not in use by some other society. They will sometimes also send individual costumes for principals for programme photo-calls at a much earlier date for a nominal fee.

With time in hand, the Wardrobe Mistress will be able to oversee her exacting office with considerable less rush and hassle, making sure that what alterations may be necessary are taken care of. There will also be time to exchange any item which is unsuitable.

With the scenery suppliers and costume suppliers being entirely different firms, it is not likely that scenery and costumes will attain the best blend of colours possible in a new production under the eye of a single Designer. With a little time in hand, however, modest changes may perhaps be made here and there. It is well worth the Director's time to make contact and establish a good relationship with the wardrobe suppliers. A personal visit if and where possible can be of great value.

Music plots

If the show is a pantomime or revue-type of production, the Director may be involved in choosing some or all of the music. He will not have the printed score to guide the Music Director, Choreographer and himself. In its place, therefore, the experienced Director will make sure there is a music plot. In all probability he will build at least the outline of this during his advance study of the proposed production.

Every piece of music required from the overture to play-out should be listed in sequence, including all songs, background music, short entrance bars, chords or whatever, with each piece numbered and a corresponding number marked in the script. In this way the Director will have a constant reminder from the script of every piece of music. This is important, especially in pantomime, for all those drum rolls, etc., used as entrance music for various characters, which have a habit of being missed out. Subsequent additions to the music plot can be indicated at the appropriate position by adding a letter to the previous cue number, e.g. 24A 'fairy entrance music', or 36B title of song. The Director will keep a copy of the plot at rehearsals and provide one for the Music Director, which he, in turn, will find useful for keeping his music in sequence.

Sequence plots

Another useful item, especially for pantomime, is the sequence plot, which is a simple list of all the items and entrances. For example:

Opening number
Baron's entrance
Robber's entrance

Rent gag
Chorus: 'Bright Day'
Dame's entrance

This should be duplicated and a copy in each dressing room will keep all concerned informed of the sequence of events especially when, as in pantomime, there may not be a strong story line dictating the numbers and changes.

The media

The society will be seeking all the publicity it can attain and there are usually good relations with the local newspaper and radio station. Often an interview (with photograph) of the Director is arranged. Journalists look for a story rather than a bland interview. It is likely that the local players will already have been covered, so it is a good idea to prepare in advance some angle either about the show and its history, or some aspect having a humorous or personal connection. Subsequent opportunities for press coverage should be welcomed.

Another aspect is the photo-call for the local press. This can be a sore point if not handled carefully. Photos in the paper are good publicity and the society needs them. What is not required is a final dress rehearsal ruined by unwanted stops for pictures of principals or ensemble. The best way is to make the photo-call on the night of the first dress rehearsal *before* the rehearsal starts. What usually happens is that the photographer will be late anyway, but because it is a stopping rehearsal, it will not prove too much of a nuisance to timing and continuity. Agree that photographers may attend the final dress rehearsal for action shots, but stress that no stops will be allowed.

The programme

The Director should check the copy to be submitted to the programme printers, especially in regard to the sequence of scenes. The list copied from the libretto may not correspond with the actual production, either because of difficulties with the scenery as supplied by the contractor, or because of changes made necessary by local staging conditions. Scenes listed that don't appear can be as irritating to spectators who follow the programme as the appearance of a front-cloth used to cover a difficult set change that isn't listed.

The Director is often expected to write a piece for the programme. Since the President and the Chairman will have their 'remarks' also, it is likely that they will have concentrated on local issues as it affects the society. Again it is a good idea to try to find a different angle of the show to write two hundred words about. Any untoward incident in the original professional production, with a comment linking it to the local production, is ideal. It often happens that some such oddity found out in this way will later appear in the reviews in the local press.

15 | *On the night*

Towards a perfect first performance

Front of house

And so the night of the first performance arrives. The foremost concern of, initially, the Director, and then the Deputy Stage-Manager, the Front-of-House Manager and the Music Director, is that the show should start *on time*. They will likewise be concerned that it should also, with a little leeway allowing for audience reaction, run to time.

The audience will react to the discourtesy of being kept waiting beyond the advertised starting time by becoming restive and if the delay is prolonged it will engender a mood of critical disparagement (or at best a kind of amused tolerance at the unprofessionalism expected of amateurs).

Apart from the effect of a late start on the audience and the increased tension to performers and production staff, there are important repercussions for management. If a professional theatre is involved, there may well be financial penalties involving overtime for orchestra, stage and front-of-house staff. The House Manager may also have arrangements with coach operators and (when traffic is a problem) the police. Repeated late starts will aggravate matters, since all concerned will begin to accept them as inevitable and thus contribute to a worsening situation.

The next thing that puts the seal of unprofessional amateurism before the show even starts is to allow anyone, however exalted a member of the society he or she may be, to gain access to either stage or auditorium via the house tabs. These should remain at all times resolutely inviolate to performers, stage staff, officials and peeping eyes.

The only excuse for delaying the curtain apart from the unexpected catastrophe or accident is a request from the Front-of-House Manager relating to the delayed arrival of large coach parties or some such other unavoidable circumstance. Co-ordination with front of house will also extend to matters such as the length of the interval, especially where there are bars or refreshment arrangements. Staff have to be informed both for actual service preparation and for public safety considerations.

Backstage

When agreement with the Front-of-House Manager has been established, the person most concerned with keeping the performance to time is the Deputy Stage-Manager. At thirty-five minutes before curtain rise, he should be in the 'corner' to announce through the public address system in the dressing-rooms and other relevant stage areas: 'This is your half-hour call.' At twenty minutes he will announce the 'fifteen minutes' call', and at ten minutes, the 'five minutes' call'. At five minutes before curtain rise it will be: 'Overture and beginners please'. By that time the Music Director should have arrived at the 'corner' to check with the Deputy Stage-Manager.

One of two alternatives usually then operates. The Deputy Stage-Manager, knowing how long it takes for the Music Director to take his place in the Orchestra pit, will give him the signal, whereupon the Music Director will make his way there and, without any further prompt, commence the overture. The other alternative is for the Music Director to take his place a little earlier, and then start after either an electronic verbal cue or a light cue from the Deputy Stage-Manager. Whichever alternative is appropriate, the last calls the Deputy Stage-Manager will make are 'curtain going up' and finally 'curtain up'. At the interval he will give a 'five minutes' call before Act Two commences.

As well as cueing the lighting, sound and stage departments, the Deputy Stage-Manager should keep a time-sheet, with scenes listed in advance, against which he may record the duration of each scene and act. This enables the Director to note the pace of the performance and is a guide for the Deputy Stage-Manager in keeping the show running to time. During the performance, hopefully with verbal communication, he will be in constant touch with all departments and so will generally be unable to leave his post. It is therefore the task of the Stage-Manager to keep an eye on what is happening on stage, before and after each scene change and generally throughout the performance.

Call-boys whose function it was to tap on dressing-room doors to advise the performers of their entrance times, have largely been superseded by strategically-placed loudspeakers, relaying the performance along the corridors and in dressing-rooms.

What the Director does

The role of the Director on the opening night should as far as possible be a passive one. Whatever heightened tensions and inner feelings build within him, he should maintain a confident calmness and appear to have all possible faith in all the company. Beyond perhaps a visit to dressing-rooms and backstage at about the half-hour call, as at the final dress rehearsal, he should stay resolutely away from backstage. His appearance there during the first performance can raise apprehension, misplaced fears and be generally disturbing and unhelpful.

The author usually hovers at the back of the stalls, often starting the applause when appropriate – it is a sad fact that viewing television at home has conditioned people not to applaud as readily as they used to in theatres, and they have to be judiciously prompted.

The curtain calls will have been arranged until the final one. At that point the Director may come to the 'corner' and judge how many calls to take and advise the Deputy Stage-Manager for future performances. On the final one he may walk in with the tabs, thank the company for their efforts and deal with any notes. He should also thank the technical people (not forgetting the Music Director who may not be backstage at that time) and take the opportunity to enquire about possible problems.

There is usually enough tension and excitement on the opening night to ensure a good trouble-free performance. It is the second night, when people having done it once feel confident enough to relax a little, that mistakes can happen. In thanking the company and technical people it is worthwhile reminding them of this tendency.

If the Director remains for the rest of the week's run, there is not a great deal more he can contribute, beyond keeping an eye on the time, checking that scenes do not spread unduly, or that the players when they relax a little do not cease to attack and drop their voices. If he has done his work well for them, he should be able to leave the company, confident that by mutual respect and effort another success can be chalked up.

GLOSSARY

Most trades and professions generate a series of terms and expressions which, while understandable to practitioners, may form an impenetrable jargon to the uninitiated. Often newcomers to a business have their ignorance of the special language exploited for the amusement of their more learned colleagues. Would-be carpenters are sometimes sent for a 'left-handed screwdriver'. Backstage, learners are sometimes sent to the theatre manager to ask for the 'key to the fly-rail'. The following limited list of terms is included not to spoil the sport of the professionals but to aid accurate communication.

ACTING AREA (1) That portion of the whole stage where the action of the performance takes place.

(2) Lanterns, usually hung immediately above, to illuminate the area where the performance is enacted.

APRON Area of stage in front of house-tabs.

BACKCLOTH (or BACKDROP) Scenic cloth which backs the setting for a performance.

BACKING Masking flat or drape set behind an opening (such as a window or door) so that the spectator does not see through to backstage or side-stage.

BACKSTAGE Area of stage behind the backcloth, or last set of lines.

BARNDOOR Metal fitment, having adjustable wings, attached to spotlight to limit spread of light.

BARREL (1) Steel tubing from which scenic items are suspended, especially in the counterweight system.

(2) (Lighting) bar from which lighting equipment is suspended. Usually hung from cables, and worked from separate winch for each bar.

BEAM-SPREAD The width of beam from a spotlight.

BORDER Curtain or other material hung across the width of the stage to hide lighting bars or tops of cloths.

BOX SET Setting for play, usually an interior, where scenic items are arranged across back and down sides of stage to form three walls. Where the fourth wall would be is left open (the imaginary fourth wall) so spectators can view the play.

BRACE Steel rod, made to support flats.

BRAIL To pass a rope from one side of the stage to the other above the borders so as to move the ropes holding the scenery from the flies, either towards the front or the back. Such a line is a brail-line.

CHANNEL Electrician's term for electrical circuit, especially one mediated by dimmer control.

CLEAT Fixture around which ropes are tied, especially row of cleats on fly-rail.

COLOUR-FILTER Transparent medium of required colour placed in front of lantern to colour the beam of light.

159

COLOUR WHEEL Disc having a number of different colour filters set in front of a spotlight. A facility to change colours easily.

CONTROL PANEL Panel of electronic switches and dimmers to activate lighting.

COUNTERWEIGHT SYSTEM A method of raising and lowering cloths, curtains and scenic items, in which the weight of the item is counter-balanced by adding on weights to a cradle.

CRADLE A kind of open cage to receive counterweights in a counterweight system.

CROSS-FADE Manipulation of lights with dimmer controls so that one lighting state is modified, more or less slowly, by introducing another lighting state, e.g. some lanterns extinguished as others are activated.

CROSS-TALK Dialogue between two persons, usually of humorous nature.

CUE Words, action or other mechanical/electrical signal to trigger subsequent action.

CUE-STATE All the lanterns activated or in use, as designated for a particular scene or effect.

CUT-CLOTH Backcloth with portions cut to conform with scenic design. When whole centre is so cut, it adds depth and perspective to a scene.

CYCLORAMA A backcloth, usually blue, set as backing to represent sky. Sometimes it is curved, sometimes made of plaster.

DEAD (1) Scenic or other items not used in current performance.
(2) Precise height or position of backcloth, curtains, flats and other scenic items for any particular scene or performance.

DEADING Arranging the correct position of scenic items for a production, especially flown items which will have a top dead, the height when flown, and a bottom dead, the position when the bottom just touches the stage.

DIMMER Instrument introduced into electrical circuit to modify the level of illumination.

DIP-TRAP Covered electrical socket set in floor of stage.

DOUBLE PURCHASE Arrangement of pulleys and lines in counterweight system which allows the weight cradle to travel only half the distance of the normal system. Used in theatres with restricted height.

DOWNSTAGE Some theatres have raked stages, i.e. sloping towards the front. Hence downstage is towards the front.

DRIFT The length of line between scenic items and the counterweight bar from which they are suspended.

EXTENDING BRACE Variable height brace to support flats.

FALSE PROSCENIUM A scenic arch set behind the house-tabs to limit the area requiring masking and to form a frame for the stage-settings.

FALSE TABS When curtains are closed on a performance as though marking the end, whereas in fact there is more to come. It is a ploy to create the impression of an encore.

FIT-UP The initial preparation and hanging of scenery prior to a production.

FLAT Wooden frame bearing stretched canvas, usually painted or dyed, as part of scenic environment.

FLIES The gallery high above the stage from which the raising and lowering of scenery is operated.

FLOATS Row of lights placed at ground level at front of stage. Name derived from original device consisting of wicks floating in trough of oil.

FLY-RAIL The rail along the front of the flies gallery, bearing cleats, to which the ropes holding the scenery, through pulleys, are tied.

FLY-TOWER The architectural height extension above the stage made necessary to accommodate the apparatus for raising scenery.

FOLLOW-SPOT Special lantern with lens system designed to facilitate a long throw, usually from front of house, to follow performer's movement on stage.

FOOTLIGHTS Row of lights at ground level placed at edge of stage – an update for floats.

FORESTAGE Area of stage in front of house-tabs – another word for apron.

FRENCH BRACE Brace hinged to flat.

FRENCH FLAT Flat with brace hinged. Also large flat battened out to give it rigidity to accommodate openings like doors or windows.

FRESNEL Spotlight with lens modified to give a soft-edged pool of light.

FRONT-CLOTH Drop-cloth set near front of stage. Often used for action while scene is changed behind.

FRONT OF HOUSE (or F.O.H.) All concerning the auditorium and theatre in front of proscenium.

GAUZE Thin, loose weaved fabric often used for vision or fade-through, dissolving effects. Opaque when lit from the front. When lights behind are faded in the scene becomes slowly visible through the gauze.

GELS Word used for colour-filters. Derived from gelatin, a material from which they were originally made.

GET-IN To bring all the paraphernalia of a production into the theatre.

GET-OUT To take a production out of the theatre.

GHOST-WALKS Term to indicate payment of salary, e.g. 'The ghost will walk at 10.30 on Friday morning'.

GOBO A metal mask with patterns cut out, placed in Profile spotlights to cast patterns of light on to stage or backcloth.

GRAVE TRAP Trap cut in the stage, originally for melodramas requiring a grave or cellar.

GREENROOM A room somewhere near the stage for actors to relax in.

GRID System of steel girders or wooden beams with pulleys, set above the stage, as part of the apparatus for raising or lowering scenery.

GROUND ROW (Scenic) A low flat set across stage, e.g. to represent a wall or hedge.

GROUND ROW (Electric) (or GROUND TROUGH) A row of lamps similar to magazine batten, used to throw light upwards, usually on a mobile mount.

HEMP-SET Flying system using hemp ropes to distinguish it from counterweight system which uses steel cables.

HOUSE LIGHTS Lights that illuminate auditorium.

HOUSE-TABS Curtains set immediately behind proscenium arch to conceal the stage from the auditorium.

IRIS Diaphragm introduced into a Profile spotlight (especially a follow-spot) which has thin metal shutters to close in or open out so as to alter the size of the circle of light cast.

LANTERN (1) Light source (usually electric lamp) enclosed in a metal housing with varying degrees of sophistication in the manner of lens, focussing, beam-spread, and angle of fixing.

(2) Stage lantern structure, to channel heat or flames in case of fire set in roof of fly-tower with windows that can be opened.

LEGS Narrow curtains at side of stage to mask off-stage areas.

LIMES Early follow-spots used lime in a flame from the combustion of oxygen and hydrogen giving an intense white light. Though replaced now by carbon-arcs or more modern lamps, they are still often known as limes.

LUMINAIRES Recently introduced term for lanterns – thought to be more readily understood world-wide.

MAROON Pyrotechnic charge to create noise of explosion.

MASKING Placing flats, curtains or borders so as to hide backstage, side-stage or above stage areas from spectators.

NEUTRALS Curtains, flats, borders of a neutral colour used in masking.

O/P (OPPOSITE PROMPT) The right-hand side of the stage, facing the audience. So named because the left side is where the Prompter is usually placed.

PATCH BOARD Electrical board usually side-stage, with sockets, allowing stage circuits to be linked temporarily to dimmer controls.

PERCH Spotlights or other lanterns placed high up, side-stage, near the front.

PERRUQUIER Specialist in wigs and hair.

PILOTS Shaded lights backstage.

PIN HINGE Device to join scenic pieces. Each half of a hinge is fastened to the scenic piece, so that when put together, they form the original hinge and are secured with a wire pin where the normal fulcrum would be.

PLOTS Lists, drawings, plans of action drawn up for the guidance of technicians and others in the course of a production.

PORTAL Flats on each side of the stage joined to a lateral flat across the top, so as to form a frame, similar to a false proscenium. It is used on deep stages to help masking.

PRE-SET Facility on lighting control board which allows one or more succeeding cue-states to be set in advance of existing cue-state.

PROFILE FLAT Flat with edge formed to blend with scenic design.

PROFILE SPOTLIGHT Spotlight which throws a hard-edged pattern of light.

PROMPT BOOK The libretto or script of a production with all necessary cues and instructions written in.

PROMPTER Person, on side of stage with script, ready to 'prompt' (i.e. speak line to actor who has forgotten it).

P/S (PROMPT SIDE) The left-hand side of the stage facing the audience. So called because the Prompter is traditionally positioned downstage there.

PROPS Short for properties, i.e. all those items necessary for a production other than scenery and costumes, including furniture, swords, sticks, bags, bottles, etc.

PROSCENIUM The wall or partition which divides the stage from the auditorium, especially the arch cut in it through which the stage is visible to the spectator.

PROSCENIUM BORDER A border set across the stage, behind the top of the proscenium arch.

PYROTECHNICS Flash, smoke, explosions and fire effects.

RISER Microphone which rises from a trap in the stage.

ROSTRUM Platform used in scenic settings to create different levels, usually made to fold.

RUNNERS Curtains on track, allowing them to open outwards from the centre.

RUNOUT Steps from auditorium to stage.

SETTING LINE Position nearest front of stage from which it is convenient to set scenery.

SIGHT-LINES The extent of the stage, at both sides and above, visible to spectators in the auditorium. This has to be known when planning the scenery. Sight-lines are ascertained by drawing a combined plan of auditorium and stage to scale and projecting lines from various spectator seat positions through the proscenium arch to the widest visible position on stage. In practice they are modified to suite the scenery by using curtains, flats and borders to mask.

SLASH Curtain made of strips of thin, glittering metallic plastic. Used to produce showy, glamorous stage dressing.

SPOT LINE Rope hung from grid at a designated spot or position.

STANDING SET Scenic setting used throughout entire play.

STAR TRAP Trap cut in stage with door made in triangular pieces the apex of each meeting at centre to form a star. Once used in mystery plays or pantomime for entrance from below or genii or demon. Rarely used now because they could be dangerous.

STRIKE To clear a stage setting.

TABS Abbreviation of tableaux curtains. Used nowadays to refer to any curtains that open or are flown.

TAB-TRACK Track from which any curtain intended to open or travel is suspended.

TALK-BACK Electronic communication facility to allow stage technicians to speak and listen to instructions or cues. Usually a headset with ear-piece and microphone.

THYRISTOR Electronic device by which lights may be dimmed.

TIE-ONS Strips of webbing sewn to cloths for tying to batten.

TRAILERS (or TRAVELLERS) Curtains that open from centre – same as runners.

TREADS Boxed-in steps to mount rostrum.

TRIPE Slang term for electric cable.

UPSTAGE (1) On raked stages the back is higher than the front, so upstage means towards the back.

(2) A trick often used by experienced players to take advantage of younger performers. It means moving further upstage, so the actor downstage has to turn his back on the audience in order to address the one upstage. In this way the audience's attention is directed away from the downstage actor to the one upstage. Nowadays it is used to refer to any occurrence which directs attention from the principal actors or performers.

U.V. Ultraviolet light (or black light). Special lamps which activate reflective power of fluorescent paint or material, so that only objects thus treated become visible on a darkened stage.

VAMP A trick door, concealed by clever painting design or other means, used to make sudden, mysterious entrances, for ghosts, vampires, etc. – hence vampire doors.

WINGS Sides of the stage hidden by flats or curtains. Such flats are sometimes called wing-flats.

WIPES (or WYPES) Curtain cloths often painted like scenic cloths which, drawn from one side, are wide enough to extend across the stage.

WORKING LIGHTS Lights to allow stage staff to set scenery. Also used during daytime working hours.

WORKING SIDE The particular side of the stage from which the Stage-Manager operates, and where tabs and other actions are worked or initiated.

RECOMMENDED READING

Plays, Scripts and Books on Theatre
Samuel French Ltd (Main Suppliers)
52 Fitzroy Street, Fitzrovia, London W1P 6JR

BOOKS

Costume

Chronicle of Western Costume, The: John Peacock, Thames and Hudson, 1991
Costume and Make-up: Michael Holt, Phaidon, 1988
Costume in the Theatre: James Laver, Harrap, 1964
Costume Reference (Period series): Marion Sichel, B. T. Batsford, 1978, 1979
Designing and Making Stage Costumes: Motley, Studio Vista, 1964
Making Costumes for Plays: J. Peters and A. Sutcliff, Harper & Row, 1977
Making Stage Costumes for Amateurs: A. V. White, Routledge, 1957
Simple Stage Costumes and How to Make Them: S. Jackson, Studio Vista, 1968
Stage Costumes: N. Lister, Jenkins, 1954
Stage Costumes and How to Make Them: Julia Tompkins, Pitman, 1978
Stage Costume Techniques: Joy Spanabel Emery, Prentice Hall, 1981
Theatrical Costume and the Amateur Stage: Arco Publications, 1968

Directing

Creative Theatre: August W. Staub, Harper & Row, 1973
Directing in the Theatre: Hugh Morrison, A. & C. Black, 1984
Fundamentals of Play Directing: Alexander Dean, Laurence Carra Holt, Rinehart
    & Winston, New York, 1974
Prospero's Staff: Charles Marowitz, Indiana University Press, 1986

Lighting

Art of Stage Lighting, The: Fredrick Bentham, Pitman, 1980
Lighting Art, The: Richard H. Palmer, Prentice Hall, 1985
Stage Lighting: Richard Pilbrow, Studio Vista, 1971
Stage Lighting Handbook (4th edition): Francis Reid, A. & C. Black, 1992

Make-up

ABC of Make-up for Men: Douglas Young, Samuel French, 1976
ABC of Make-up for Women: Douglas Young, Samuel French, 1976
Book of Make-up: E. Ward, Samuel French, 1933
Face is a Canvas, The: Irene Corey, Anchorage Press, 1990

Practical Stage Make-up: T. Perotter, Studio Vista, 1968.
Stage Make-up (6th edition): Richard Corson, Prentice Hall, London, 1970
Theatrical Make-up: Bert Broe, Pelham Books, 1992

Props

Come Down Stage: Susan Date & Kelvin Watson, Pelham Books, 1971
Create Your Own Stage Props: Jacquie Govier, A. & C. Black, 1984
Make-up, Masks and Wigs: C. Ray Smith (ed.) Whiteline Publications, 1974
Stage Properties: Heather Conway, Herbert Jenkins, 1959
Stage Props and How to Make Them: W. Kenton, Pitman, 1964

Sound

Lighting and Sound: Neil Fraser, Phaidon, Oxford, 1988
Sound For The Stage: Patrick M. Finelli, Drama Book Publishers, 1989
Sound For The Theatre: Graham Walne, A. & C. Black, 1990
Stage Sound: David Collison, Cassell, 1982

Stage Craft

Here's How: Herbert V. Make, Samuel French, 1958
An Introduction to Scenic Design: A. S. Gillette, Harper & Row, 1967
Stage Management: Hal D. Stewart, Pitman, 1957
Stage Management: Lawrence Stern, Allyn & Bacon, 1974
Stage Management, A Gentle Art: Daniel Bond, A. & C. Black, 1991

PERIODICALS

Amateur Theatre (monthly); also Year Book: Platform Publications Ltd, 83 George St, London W1H 5PL. Tel. 0171 486 1732.

Contacts and *Spotlight Casting Directory* (both yearly): 7 Leicester Place, London WC2H 7BP. Tel. 0171 437 7631.

Lights (three times a year and free): Strand Lighting Ltd, Grant Way, Syon Lane, Isleworth, Middlesex TW7 5QD. Tel. 0181 560 3171.

Noda News (each Spring and September): NODA, 1 Crestfield St, London WC1. Tel. 0171 837 5655.

Stage and Television Today (weekly): 47 Bermondsey St, London SE1 3XT. Tel. 0171 403 1818. Published on Thursdays, available at most newsagents. This is the profession's only newspaper and has a directory section of suppliers and services for the theatre.

USEFUL ADDRESSES

SUPPLIERS

Costumiers

Charles Alty, 173 Lees Road, Oldham, Lancs. Tel. 0161 620 0898.

Bermans M. Ltd., 18 Irving St, London WC2H 7AX. Tel. 0171 839 1651.

Costume Workshop, 43 High St, Shanklin, Ise of Wight, PO37 7JJ. Tel. 0193 866 650.

Paul Craig (millinery), Unit 3, Wealden Business Park, Farningham Rd, Crowborough, E. Sussex TN6 2JR. Tel. 01892 667 949.

Charles H. Fox, 22 Tavistock St, Covent Garden, London WC2E 7PY. Tel. 0171 240 3111.

The Haslemere Wardrobe, St Christopher's Rd, Haslemere, Surrey GU27 1DQ. Tel. 01428 642 202.

Homburgs, King House, Regent St, Leeds LS2 7UZ. Tel. 01532 458425.

Lyndon Theatrical Costume Hire, 42 High St, West Mersea, Colchester, Essex CO5 8JX. Tel. 01206 384 471.

Midland Costume, Unit 10, Scott Lidgett Rd, Longport, Stoke-on-Trent ST6 4NQ. Tel. 01782 822 875.

Morris Angel Ltd, 119 Shaftesbury Avenue, London WC2H 8AE. Tel. 0171 836 5678.

Northern Costume Hire, 16 Swadford St, Skipton, North Yorkshire. Tel. 01756 790 526.

Taylor-Maid Costumes, 550 Hessle Rd, Hull, North Humberside HU3 5BL. Tel. 01482 219 159.

Theatrical Costume House (Westcliff) Ltd, 83 Brunswick Rd, Southend-on-Sea, Essex SS1 2UL. Tel. 01702 461 573.

Utopia Costumes, 229 Tarring Rd, Worthing, West Sussex BN11 4HG. Tel. 01903 504 226/784 628.

Lighting

Lanterns, fixtures, rigging, effects and all accessories:

Strand Lighting Ltd, Grant Way, Syon Lane, Isleworth, Middlesex TW7 5QD. Tel. 0181 560 3171.

CCT, Hindle House, Traffic Street, Nottingham NG2 1NE. Tel: 01602 862722.

Scenic projectors and effects:

David Mersey Associates Ltd, 15 Between Streets, Cobham, Surrey KT1 1AA. Tel. 01932 7117.

Second-hand and refurbished lighting for hire and sale:

David Fitch Services, Unit 5, Northend Industrial Estate, Northend Rd, Erith, Kent DA8 3PP. Tel. 01322 350 351.

Make-up

Charles H. Fox, 22 Tavistock St, Covent Garden, London WC2E 7PY. Tel. 0171 240 3111.
Make-up Centre, 26 Bute St, London SW7 3EX. Tel. 0171 584 2188.
NODA, 1 Crestfield St, London WC1. Tel. 0171 837 5655.

Props

All Sorts of Props, 31A St Johns Park, London SE3 7JW. Tel. 0181 858 9834.
Howorth Wrightson Ltd, The Prop House, Unit 2, Cricket St, Denton, Manchester M34 3DR. Tel. 0161 335 0220.
Leon Cooper, 10-14 Station Rd, Batley, West Yorkshire. Tel. 01924 475 057.
Prop Workshops Ltd, 43 High St, New Malden, Surrey KT3 4BY. Tel. 0181 942 6533.
Richard Hewer, 7 Sion Lane, Clifton, Bristol BS8 4BE. Tel. 0117 973 8760.

Scenery hire

Scenery, properties, furniture:

Border Studio, Forest Mill, Dunsdale Rd, Selkirk TD7 5AA. Tel. 01750 20237.
Dennis Williams Scenic and Property Hire, Unit 5A, Cambrian Industrial Estate, Coedcae Lane, Pontyclun, Mid. Glam. CF7 9EW. Tel. 01443 237 590.
James Fredricks, Scenic Studios, Langford Rd, Weston-super-Mare, Avon. Tel. - 1934 624 791.
Stagesets, Unit L, Delta Wharf, Blackwall Industrial Estate, Tunnel Avenue, Greenwich, London SE10 0QH. Tel. 0181 835 2370.
The Stage Productions Co Ltd, Caslough Centre, Eley Industrial Estate, Nobel Rd, Edmonton, London N18 3BH. Tel. 0181 803 1779.
Top Show, Unit 6, Acaster Malbis Indusrial Estate, York YO2 1XB. Tel. 01904 701 611.

Scenic materials

Canvas, paints, colours, brushes:

Brodie & Middleton Ltd, 68 Drury Lane, London WC2B 5SP. Tel. 0171 836 3289/3280.

J. D. McDougall Ltd, 4 McGrath Rd, Stratford, London E14 4JP. Tel. 0181 534 2921.

Rosco, Roscolab Ltd, Blanchard Works, Kangley Bridge Rd, London SE26 5AQ. Tel. 0181 659 2300.

Russell & Chapple Ltd, 23 Monmouth St, Shaftesbury Avenue, London WC2H 9DE. Tel. 0171 836 7521.

Sound

Alpha Audio, Unit 5, Brookland Close, Sunbury-on-Thames, Middlesex TW16 7DX. Tel. 01932 765 550.

The Music Company, Bradford. Tel. 01274 370 966.

Theatre Sound & Lighting (Services) Ltd, 67 Drury Lane, London WC2B 5SP. Tel. 0171 836 7877.

Sound effects

BBC Sound Effects, London W1A 1AA (or record shops).

Samuel French Ltd, 52 Fitzroy St, London W1P 6JR. Tel. 0171 387 9373.

Special stage dressings

Glitter, plastic mirror, metallic PVC, shimmer materials:

Chris James & Co Ltd, 19 New Wharf Rd, London N1 9RT. Tel. 0171 837 3062/3.

N. & I. Costello, 225 Red Lion Rd, Tolworth, Surbiton, Surrey KT6 7RF. Tel. 0181 397 7830.

Roscolab Ltd, Blanchard Works, Kangley Bridge Rd, London SE26 5AQ. Tel. 0181 659 2300.

Stage fittings

Tab tracks, hardware, braces, pulleys:

Flint Hire and Supply Ltd, Queens Road, London SE17 2PX. Tel. 0171 703 9786.

Halls Stage Products, The Gate Studios, Station Rd, Boreham Wood, Herts WD6 1DQ. Tel. 0181 953 9371.

Wigs

A. & A. Hair Studios, 8-10 Tanfield, Inverleith, Edinburgh EH3 5HF. Tel. 0131 556 7057.

Derek Easton, 1st Floor, 19 Wardour St, London W1V 3HD. Tel. 0171 439 1366.

Warren Landsfield, 47 Glenmore Rd, Hampstead, London Tel. 0171 722 4581.
Wig Creations, 62 Lancaster Mews, London W2 3QG. Tel. 0171 402 4488.

THE NATIONAL OPERATIC AND DRAMATIC ASSOCIATION (NODA)

With an affiliation of 2,300 amateur theatre societies and a further membership of 2,200 individual members, NODA is the largest association representing amateur theatre in Britain. Its headquarters are at 1 Crestfield Street, London WC1H 8AU. Telephone 0171 837 5655. It is organised into twelve regional areas which elect representatives to area conferences, a National Conference and an Annual General Meeting. A separate trading company, NODA Ltd, sells new scores, libretti, and playscripts, holds the rights to over fifty pantomimes, and acts as the agent and insurance agent for societies. There is a quarterly national newspaper, plus area news bulletins and directories. NODA organises three annual residential summer schools for actors, singers, directors and technicians. There is helpful, friendly service at the headquarters, ready to advise affiliated societies in emergency.

Index